got dessert?

MARSHMALLOW

In sorgfältiger, detailverliebter Handar...
und aus besten (Bio) Produkten hergestel...

A Delicious Life

NEW FOOD ENTREPRENEURS

gestalten

New explorers, new frontiers

Let's face it. Food is an everyday temptation—and an every-day need. And for some, it has even become an everyday obsession: a quality driven obsession for those who are looking for meaning, cultural heritage, or consistency in the produce they come across. Take bread for example. It comes in all sorts of shapes, can be made from a wide variety of flours, and reflects all kinds of traditions. From a French baguette to a German pumpernickel or a Chinese steamed bun, bread is more than a staple food. A currency in ancient times and a cornerstone of many cultures, it is now also being looked upon with innovation thanks to a new genera-tion of bakers who are revisiting old techniques and sourc-ing stone-pressed flours to craft great loaves. Whether it is chocolate or bread, yogurt or tea, basic products are being embraced by chefs and foodies, who are steadily bringing them to new levels. The new coffee culture is yet another example of self-reinvention. Available worldwide, and with brands like Nespresso bringing portioned, uniform pods to the masses, coffee has many varied cultural expres-sions and tastes depending on the region. In Italy call it a ristretto at the counter, in Turkey call it a murky khave, and in a new coffee shop in Brooklyn, Portland, or Oslo, a single-origin coffee is taken very seriously and flavors reach new heights through impeccable roasting and sophisticated filtering processes such as Chemex or Siphon. The same attention to detail occurs when crafting chocolate and bitters, ice creams, and baked goods. All are rediscovered by a generation of self-taught chefs and passionate food-en-trepreneurs who explore produce, source ingredients, and reinvent cooking as if they were new frontiers.
Following these footsteps, a new generation of food craft-ers is taking the lead. And the most striking thing about them venturing forward is that they do so by looking back, by unearthing old recipes and produce. Whatever the product, the trend has become global in reassessing the quality of a handpicked tea, digging into an old-fashioned macaron recipe, and exploring new creative outcomes in making ice cream, butter, mustard, etc. There isn't one pantry item that isn't being rediscovered and taken to a new level of taste through creativity.
Even agriculture is redefining its role in certain regions. Have you heard of boreal agriculture or gastronomic agriculture? Coined by Montreal-based culinary company Société-Orignal, the latter looks at agriculture under a new light. Agriculture should be Basic-Unique. "Our maple syrups and honey jars come in limited editions because we work with real farmers. We work following simple, con-sistent principles and most importantly, we don't try to push the limits of nature. We'd rather concentrate on the unknown, on crafting great local products that no one has thought about, like for our Gaspésie honey. By transport-ing the beehives near the St. Lawrence estuary, we expose the bees to constant sea-winds, which they convert into a strong saltwater flavor. Our honey is salty," they explain. "We love how such products speak about the terroir of northern Quebec. It's so Canadiana, so wild, rare, and pure."

Resetting the timeline

After a glorious decade of fusion food, during which all kinds of high-flung products from around the world ended up in the same dish—a bit like an executive team of inter-national CFOs meeting over figures, but dragging with them more jetlag and carbon footprint than common sense—the time for this has wound down. The time in which to as-sess local resources as true gold and reevaluate produce in regard to seasons has arrived. Back to old days and old recipes, we are resetting and recalibrating the timeline. We need to think like our grandparents did, unearth forgotten root vegetables, and go foraging for mushrooms, berries, and seaweed. Take three-Michelin-star-chef Alain Passard for example. Not only does he run two kitchen gardens, plus a fruit orchard, but he harvests his own vegetables, which include 70 to 80 varieties of tomatoes and beets in all colors—red, white, yellow, pink, and even zebra. Going north, following the footsteps of world-acclaimed chef René Redzepi, leads us to further explore the roots of Nordic cuisine through the carefully appointed Nordic Food Lab. And, on a day-to-day basis, one can simply talk to the anonymous mushroom forager who comes to the local farmers' market every week, with baskets of nettles at times and wild flowers at others. Clearly standing out, a new generation of chefs, farmers, and artisans are driven by the quality and originality of what they can grow or forage; some in a vanguard way, others with scrutiny and common sense, all converging in the end. Returning to the example of New Nordic Cuisine proves very informative. "The movement has, to a large extent, been shaped by the Manifesto for a New Nordic Cuisine, published by a group of Scandinavian chefs in 2004, creating a new food discourse based on produce only grown within the Nordic region," Mark Emil Hermansen, Anthropologist at Nordic Food Lab explains. "By (re)creating a Nordic terroir, New Nordic Cuisine enables its natives to ingest the cultural landscape, and consume a material version of local and regional identity." Further quoting artist Gordon Matta-Clark, who said "cuisine is not food, it is food transcended, nature transformed into a social product" (1975), Hermansen proves that the reason cuisine is so interesting is that it's pure anthropology. Food trends are pure anthropology.

In the digital era, people have become more nomadic; so has food

A digital expert would comment that food trucks have gone viral. Clustered around city centers and dense urban environments, they offer instant great quality food to busy crowds. If cities like New York or Sydney have developed their own food truck apps, others are using them as a powerful socio-cultural tool. As part of its European Cultural Capital 2013 program, Marseille has unveiled a series of thirteen designed Grandes Carrioles (Large Carts) that will tour the city serving different kinds of experimental cooking. "Even if they are playful, the carts will serve great food and echo the pleasure of walking around farmers' markets where one can sample, on-the-go, fresh produce and terroir specialties. It's all about sharing and reestablishing quality, on wheels," the mayor explains. Matching our new eating habits, kitchens are changing, increasingly designed to be mobile. Nomad kitchenettes and new storage facilities have become more modular to follow our needs, serving as outdoor barbecues at times and indoor cooking pods at others. Even kitchen tools are evolving to save time, highlight lost cultural practices, or encourage sustainability and different kinds of cooking methods. Isabelle Mathez, for example, developed Malle W. Trousseau, an expert's cooking trunk that gathers great tools from all around the world, after realizing that her 18-year-old daughter was leaving the house and wanting to take the chopping board and knife she had grown up with. "Retrospectively it was obvious. Our daughter had grown up with these objects and they were as much a part of her life as they were of ours. To take them with her was to take part of her family and the rituals that had surrounded her since she was a child, so it seemed only natural to do so. The idea of putting together a trousseau for her began to take form at around that time. Not the sort of trousseau that our grandmothers might have been presented with on getting married, with its tablecloths and embroidered sheets, but a collection of practical utensils that would last her a lifetime, that would be meeting her practical needs for a lifetime," Isabelle Mathez recalls.

People need to reconnect with the land and their roots; so does food

Following the impact of the New Nordic Cuisine movement on world gastronomy, the Cook It Raw Festival was started by Rene Redzepi's ex-executive chef, Alessandro Porcelli, and journalist Andrea Petrini in 2009 as a response to molecular cuisine and the industry's soaring carbon footprint. To illustrate its philosophy, and the idea of belonging to a land, the festival states that it will do the same as what Czeslaw Milosz expressed in his "Wherever" poem. "Wherever I am, at whatever place on earth, I hide from people the conviction that I'm not from here. It's as if I'd been sent, to extract as many colors, tastes, sounds, smells, to experience everything that is a man's share, to transpose what was felt into a magical register and carry it there, from whence I came." The strong idea of carrying something home—a memory, a taste, a dish—is also what guided Lebanese-born Kamal Mouzawak to found Tawlet, a farmer's kitchen that works with skilled grandmothers and experienced local farmers to revisit past recipes. Tawlet brings back to downtown Beirut the sense of belonging to a community, to a land, to a culture. It acts as a new kind of counterculture.

People need to find new grounds for experimenting and mixing influences; so does food

Today, stepping into one's neighborhood gourmet store, one may find a homemade hearty soup of the day for those in search of mom's comfort food; a disguised kale-quinoa vegan-meets-vegetarian salad for those who've turned their lives into a healthy organic quest; regional artisanal cheese and cured meats; farm-grown seasonal produce; and delicacies sampled from around the world, from French pure-origin chocolate or sugarless Japanese sweets to Manuka honey from New Zealand. For collectors of fine foods selecting the best of the best, neighborhood gourmet stores are not only thinking fresh and local, but are growing in their dedication to quality and diversity. They are a reflection of our quest for cultural diversity in food. Following the same pattern, local neighborhood restaurants are mixing influences to cater to new needs. For example, New York's Asiadogs revisits a local favorite with Asian flair. By topping hotdogs with flavors found in China, Korea, Vietnam, and Japan, they celebrate New York City's diversity with a twist. The future of food, from the most basic product to the most sophisticated restaurant concept, will be about regaining biodiversity.

People have even become sick with food and are now trying to detox

By his description, Marcus Antebi, founder of super-healthy concept Juice Press, was born in the age of cookie crisp and Captain Crunch cereals sold as part of "a complete breakfast." "My parents fed me processed corn and mountains of sugar floating in a bowl of pasteurized cow milk. A disgrace and a tragedy! It took me 20 years to break the terrible addiction to processed foods and refined sugars." Almost three decades later, Antebi has been 27 years sober: no dairy, no soy, lots of green juice, and a diet consisting of 90% raw food with a small amount of cooked veggies once or twice a week. The story seems radical but many of us who are part of "Generation Y" are surrounded by friends who converted to raw food or became lactose intolerant overnight, or by colleagues who turned to vegan diets and entrepreneurs like Jesper Rydahl, Danish founder of 42° Raw, who changed his approach to food to bring us a healthy, sustainable proposal. We went from "yes to all" to "no to all," and as we are consistently freeing ourselves from gluten and lactose, GMOs and hormones, a new type of frontier is emerging called barren food.

In this new promising land, health and food are

intertwined, not for medical purposes, but more as a life-enhancer. Healthy foods are as much about pleasure and feeling one's best as they are curative. They are about the sense of feeling younger.

Food is changing, so are people

Once forgotten, farmers' markets and pocket-sized gourmet stores have sprung back into city centers. Though French bakeries have always been around, there came a point when most of them were selling baguettes using prepared flour mix or semi-industrialized bread. But as food started to cater to a handful of uncompromised foodies—those willing to spend much more on an organic loaf and heirloom tomatoes, on fresh farm butter and handmade cakes—the offers really changed, reaching out to a new generation of sophisticated urban connoisseurs and amateurs. People started designing their own kitchens and making a detour to pick up a real cheese plate from a cheesemonger or a biodynamic bottle of wine. This radical change in our attitude toward food—the complete opposite of good value for the money—is linked to education. The foodies are educating us to choose right, learn about produce and the producers, and pay for its real value like one pays extra for additional content or for an exhibition. And by triggering knowledge about food, foodies are nurturing the idea that nature is behind it all, and accessible to all. They highlight that fields and farms can be in close reach of the city, that communal gardens and rooftop herb gardens should spring up on every corner, that a beehive in the city is a healthy sign, and that kids should have gardening lessons at school and learn that eggs reconstructed out of powder aren't the same as those laid by chickens. Changing our attitude toward the urban environment, foodies are cracking up concrete areas with vegetable gardens. They are using every available urban interstice to bring nature back into our modernized world.

People have become lonely, so has food

As our society has grown anonymous, so has food. Stepping into a Starbucks, whether it be on a mainstream avenue, in a mall, or in an airport, will never give the feeling of a neighborhood coffee shop. The sense of belonging to a community, although this remains a subjective feeling, is intensely linked to names—to the luxury of addressing the owner or regulars by name. Naming the producer also differentiates mass-produced food from local farms. A recent French initiative called Le Petit Producteur, which brings baskets of seasonal fruits and vegetables to local supermarket Monoprix, quickly stands out, as each basket bears the name, the region, and a picture of the producer that grew it. Humanizing food, linking it back to a region, a terroir, and a place is a huge part of the food trend to reconnect with sound basis and earthy products. Even chocolatiers and coffee roasters discuss the finca and estates from which they've sourced the beans. Grocers are giving products a sense of place, choosing to handwrite the provenance of a tomato or piece of meat on a blackboard instead of sticking an anonymous barcode on the back of the product. This raises the real issue of modern traceability. How modern does it need to be? There is no need to trace the provenance of peaches at a farmers' market in Luberon, Provence, in the summer. You can feel it when you weigh them, and sense that they still hold sun and have been picked just hours before. But when you are faced with aisles of groceries and processed foods in supermarkets, tracing back their origin becomes a very sensitive issue. Will producers end up winning ground over big corporations? Will good food sign the death of barcodes? From what I know, there's never been a barcode in genuine, local French bakeries: baguettes come only with a name.

Time for Bread

◊ Bread has been one of the principal forms of food for man
since the earliest of times. Björn Schwind's Zeit für Brot
takes us back to basics and reminds us that the simple
things in life are usually best. A trained master baker
and business economist, Schwind recognizes the value
of traditional customer-oriented bakeries. His first bake
house and deli opened in Frankfurt in 2009, and a second
one followed about three years later in Berlin. True to
its name, Zeit für Brot (Time for Bread) counters the fast
food mentality of bakery chains and discounters in favor
of implementing good old virtues such as craftsmanship
and comfort. Reviving Western Europe's rich heritage in
bread-making, Zeit für Brot reintroduces bread as an
essential part of daily social life. It offers what the modern
world appears to lack: a comfortable place to sit back
and enjoy fine organic bread paired with nice chats at
◊ large rustic tables.

Six distinctively different flavors of golden nectar from Lebanon

◇ Beirut-based designer Karen Chekerdjian is passionate about olive oils, and believes
Lebanon has some of the most flavorsome and well-produced bottles. A few months
back, she started sourcing and selecting extra virgin olive oils from five Lebanese
family-run domains across four contrasting Lebanese regions—Fattal, Metni, Antar,
Zahad, Kohor. A few intense tasting sessions later, she narrowed down her choice to
six olive oils based on their inherent quality, level of acidity, unique blend, organic
approach, or the traditional stone-disk pressing method used to extract them.
Karen then picked a dark-tinted glass bottle from Italy—designed to preserve the
oils from direct sunlight—and created a graphic identity that would best translate
the quality of the golden nectar. The result is six exquisite olive oils that contain
◇ six different fragrances from the Lebanese soil.

PD: 02102012

feinschlicht

Gemüseaufstrich

Zwiebel & Portwein

Balsam für die Zwiebelseele

Inhalt: 170 g | Gemüseanteil- und Frucht 63%

Zutaten: 69% Zwiebeln*, 15% Roh-

Feinschlicht

Small glasses carry big flavors

The art of canning and preserving has been forgotten in recent decades, replaced by industrial methods that destroy the bright flavors of real fruits and vegetables. Falko Schumann, who has a deep commitment to reminding people what they've been missing, studied nutritional sciences and worked as a chef in Munster before moving to Berlin, where he started Feinschlicht in 2011. It is here that he sells the vegetable spreads, chutneys, oils, vinegars, and salts that he makes by hand from local and organic produce without the addition of artificial coloring, preservatives, or flavor enhancers.

The finest and rarest Sicilian olive oil in Paris

Cédric Casanova is a dreamer. Better, he's a storyteller. In his world, every olive has a name, a personality: la biancolilla is light and discreet while la cerasuola is slightly peppery, vigorous, and la nocellera del belice intense, green and, at times, even bitter. Think of them as noble heiresses or antique goddesses.

With his heart in Syracuse and his feet in his pocket-sized Parisian boutique, former tightrope circus artist Cédric Casanova fills his Sicilian host's table with the best of Sicily (olives, capers, almonds, homemade sundried tomato-almond-tuna pasta, exceptional tuna bresaola). He keeps it so authentic that within month of opening he had Michelin-star chefs coming to him to stock up on authentic Italian produce. Soon after, he was awarded Le Fooding's Best Table d'Hôte in 2011. But if the table speaks about rural Sicilian fare, the shelves are what make the trip to rue Ste Marthe really worthwhile. Stacked with cans of olive oils, they hold a Sicilian history of climate and sun-drenched harvesting moments. First, every olive oil bears the name of its producer—Marco, Paola, Francesco—someone Casanova knows and has personally worked with in Sicily. Second, every olive oil is different for it reflects a terrain, a climate, and the nature of the olive-press. Third, the olive oils he sells are so noble that they simply cannot be categorized, patented, or standardized.

"I don't grade the olive oils," Casanova explains. "Each family has its olive grove where they have always produced olive oils for themselves. It's a part of them, of their land. Olive oil is part of the family. When you craft a final product as beautiful as this, it's like your son. Would you care if someone applied standards to your son? Of course not! It's your son. You will still love him and be proud of him. Each oil is like the farmer's child. Every yearly harvest is like a new dawn, a new (and very tasty) chapter. And they will sell some to you only if they have extra."

On the shelf, one can read "ALFP—total production of 67 kg," which means, like a wine label, that this extra virgin olive oil is made by the Alfano family (hence the ALF) using only piricuddara olives (hence the P). But there is more to this tiny batch than a Sicilian sticker and a family name. "The Alfano family is like a clan: three brothers and a father, in the field. When I scouted their land, I found 12 very ancient piricuddara olive trees. They hadn't been pruned for some time but they looked vigorous. Altogether we decided to put them back into business, and the first olives we pressed had a slight pistachio taste. Can life get better than this?" Casanova recalls. Following Casanova's steps into his 14 m² boutique is like traveling across Sicily, discovering Felicia's cerasuola olive trees (an antique Etruscan variety), which produce an oil with a distinctive carob aroma, or Katia's oliveraie, where she first greeted Casanova with a tongue-in-cheek "Are you the Olive Oil Man? Because if it's you, your eyes have the same color as my olives." He blushed and a moment later was invited to taste their olive oil. To this day he recalls the artichoke flavors that came out of the green oil.

And back to the exceptional quality of hand-harvested, family-run olive groves. "If you think buying 'extra virgin' labeled olive oil makes a difference, you are wrong. There are no standards whatsoever for olive oils," he comments. And as is also the case for many other products, knowing the producer, or even better, buying produce with the name of the farmer or harvester attached to it, is the best label one can find. The same principle is valid at any honest farmer's market where tomatoes, apples, and fresh goat cheese aren't labeled, standardized, or marketed; they are simply ripe or sweet, milkier or stronger. The farmer will tell you about the hale storm and how the past dry summer months have made the figs so sweet—a humbling lesson that links the produce back to the soil and the hand that farms it.

Every olive oil tin on Cédric Casanova's shelves is an example of this: a legend of its own that cannot be reproduced and will never really taste the same two years in a row. Every olive oil has its personality, like a good book has unique characters. Tasting olive oils at La Tête dans les Olives is like reading a good book, with "one's head perched high in the olive tree."

a tête dans
Huile d'olive
PRODUITS DE SICILE
GROS, ½ GROS, DÉTAIL
EPICERIE
FROMAGES

Charlito's Cocina

The essence of curing meats

◊ Charles Samuel Wekselbaum grew up in New York City in a Cuban-American household where he learned that traditional methods of food preservation have an important place in the modern kitchen. He was educated at the French Culinary Institute in New York City and was mentored by two chefs who produced much of their own charcuterie. After graduation he lived with family in Salamanca and Extremadura, Spain, where he learned their tradition of curing meats and olives and making wine. After years of training, Wekselbaum opened Charlito's Cocina in 2011, where he slowly prepares everything from scratch using heritage-breed pork that is 100% pasture-raised, which leaves time to experiment with new recipes and products.
◊

Smoke on the water

◊ Glut und Späne is Berlin's first sustainable fish smokery. Long before its doors opened in 2012, founder Michael Wickert began learning the tradition of fish smoking as he traveled the world. Beginning as a graduate student of aquaculture and fishery sciences in Berlin, he went on to explore inshore fisheries in Brazil and salmon aquaculture and hand-fishing in Norway. He researched abalone in South Africa and worked on a family-run trout farm and restaurant in Switzerland. It was in Normandy, while managing three trout farms and developing recipes inspired by the region, that he had the idea to open his own fish smokery. Glut und Späne reinterprets the tradition of fish smoking by combining his international recipe collection with his immense ◊ passion for fish.

Kaiser Honig

Inner-city honey bees

After a trip to the Amazon, Kristian Kaiser became interested in the ancient methods that used honey to preserve herbs. He began combining milk and honey with ingredients like sesame, vanilla, coconut, and cacao to create an unusual brand of honey he called Kaiser Honey. Today, the business is housed in an old factory building in Berlin, a city whose Turkish and Vietnamese cultures have had an important influence on his products. As a honey maker and beekeeper, the recent global devastation of bee colonies has taken on personal meaning; it reinforces Kaiser's commitment to producing on a small-scale with sustainable ingredients that protect the bee population and the environment.

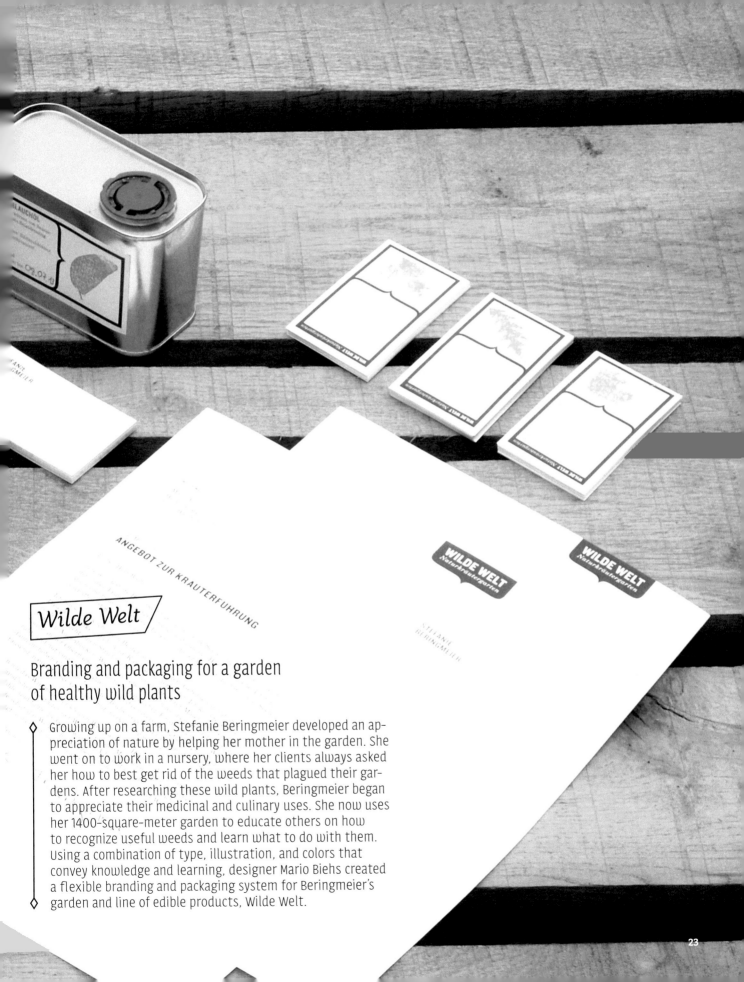

ANGEBOT ZUR KRAUTERFUHRUNG

Wilde Welt

Branding and packaging for a garden of healthy wild plants

Growing up on a farm, Stefanie Beringmeier developed an appreciation of nature by helping her mother in the garden. She went on to work in a nursery, where her clients always asked her how to best get rid of the weeds that plagued their gardens. After researching these wild plants, Beringmeier began to appreciate their medicinal and culinary uses. She now uses her 1400-square-meter garden to educate others on how to recognize useful weeds and learn what to do with them. Using a combination of type, illustration, and colors that convey knowledge and learning, designer Mario Biehs created a flexible branding and packaging system for Beringmeier's garden and line of edible products, Wilde Welt.

Got Dessert?

Homemade fluffy fresh confections

◇ Stacey Horn began baking professionally
when a friend opened an organic food store in
Berlin. Brownies and cheesecakes were her first
creations, soon followed by an experiment with
making homemade marshmallows. Fascinated
by the transformation of sugar into wonderfully
fluffy and fresh confections, and blown away by
how good fresh marshmallows tasted compared
to their industrial counterparts, she began
making marshmallows in flavors like chocolate
and vanilla raspberry puree. Got Dessert was
born. Now she sells marshmallows along with
her other baked goods at the local market in
◇ Berlin's Friedrichshain neighborhood.

Astarism Food Design

Radical new visual presentations of classical dishes

◇ Dynamic pairings of design and food are at the heart of Andrew
Stellitano's work. His sensibilities were set into motion when he
began working in commercial kitchens at the age of 17, and later
as a graphic design student at Central Saint Martins in London.
As a professional food designer, his meticulously researched
projects combine historical recipes with modern techniques.
His clients include brands such as Gucci and Lyle's Golden Syrup,
for whom he created Panscapes, a series based on classic recipes
that transform the flat topography of traditional pancakes
◇ into theatrical landforms.

The brotherhood of chocolate makers

"We were roommates for four or five years, but we've been brothers our whole lives." Known as the Mast Brothers, the ambassadors of handcrafted American chocolate, Rick and Michael Mast always present themselves with a hint of humor. Anchored in a nondescript building in Williamsburg, their story unfolds as a page in a history book, when explorers sailed the world to source the best cocoa beans and spices. Following those adventurous journeys, the Mast Brothers like to see their chocolate factory as a world of atlases and unknown territories, channeling the love of adventure on which they built their brand. Stepping inside, one is greeted by jute bags freshly shipped from the four corners of the globe, old glass jars, brick walls painstakingly restored, and carefully wrapped chocolate bars lined up on wooden shelves behind an old counter. And to spice it up, the brothers' two long reddish beards and old-school looks bring any visitor back a few decades.

"Every step of the way, we've had to come up with how it's done. There is no such thing (in the US) as small-batch chocolate makers. There is no such thing as a chocolate kit," say the brothers. From the start, chocolate was for them the perfect produce to explore, as it arguably remains one of the most popular foods on earth, and yet no one knows how it's made. "There is no magic; to have a bean reach its full flavor potential, it has to be done small. If you take the best bean, you're going to get the best product," they explain. Doing everything themselves, The Mast Brothers start by opening the bag on their butcher block table and hand-sorting every bean. Each bean then gets a different roasting profile. And they do it craft style, which means there is no room for anything other than cocoa bean and sugar in their bars; they don't add any additional vegetable oils, cocoa butter, vanilla, or soy lecithin. "We highlight the cocoa bean, its origin,

and its natural flavors by breaking up the beans by hand, using a machine that was developed by a friend of ours, an aerospace engineer. It's usually used by home brewers to break up barley," they add. After being in the stone grinder for 2–3 days, the beans are then ready to rest for a couple of weeks before going through a tempering process that brings the chocolate to its perfect melting point. Hence, a perfect bar.

"Cacao beans were used as currency by the Aztec centuries ago. They were known as the food of Gods. Following such ancient history, we always try to stay as close as possible to the roots of chocolate and cacao beans; the driving force in our project was for us to re-connect with our curiosity and master the art of crafting chocolate." And it was probably this same curiosity for the unknown that appealed to the great explorers when they set sail to Madagascar and Sao Tomé, across the

world atlas of cacao beans. "We've always been on the lookout for new ideas; we were challenged by the excitement to rediscover chocolate."

"And we always get our hands dirty, whether it's building something from scratch, going somewhere we've never been before, or meeting someone new. So we naturally question everything that we do, from sourcing the beans to handcrafting our bars," they add.

"Everything in our enterprise roots back to our love affair with the spirit of craft and things that are crafted. That is why you'll find us restoring an old letterpress printer to emboss wooden sailboats or vintage blueprints into our thick wrapping paper, and we deliver every hand-wrapped slab as if it were a rare book."

"As your taste buds learn more and more about chocolate, they leap forward. Subsequently, tasting chocolate for us is like old Mark Twain stories. It speaks about

adventure, independence, and a fierce spirit of freedom." With an old-school literary approach, the Mast Brothers are writing their own story as they go. Crafting their own bar is like a voyage into the unknown, which they write for themselves, their friends, and a dedicated community of followers. "Chocolate itself represents more than just a candy bar. It symbolizes a new way of handcrafting food, an old mentality or way of doing things that is modern again. And way beyond our belief, it's spreading like wild fire, the same way our horizon has opened up tremendously, as brothers."

And if you question them about going into business as brothers, they answer: "There is nobody that you're going to fight harder against than your family, but nobody that you're going to fight harder for than your family."

When cocoa beans meet spices

Ecuadorian Sebastián Cisneros came to the United States with more in mind than just business studies. After working shifts in Portland's landmark Cacao store, Cisneros soon decided to reconnect with his South American origins, and started crafting chocolate from home. Cocanú, a line of sleek, tile-shaped bars, was born. Featuring complex combinations of spices and single-origin beans, he introduced cayenne, ginger, pimentón, and coconut into his bars. If the spicy Picasso square infuses a rare raw, dark strain made by Picari in Ecuador with cayenne and smoked paprika, then the truly fascinating marriage comes from dark chocolate infused with bits of smoky Ecuadorian Palo Santo wood, usually burnt in churches. The blend surprisingly unveils dill flavors. Cocanú? "Chocolate dreams maneuvered in Portland, Oregon," as mentioned on the ecofriendly pulp-paper packaging.

MOONWALK

SINDY
by cocanú CHOCOLATE

33

Paletas

Ice cream as we want it

◇ Authentic Mexican paletas are the ultimate slow food; made by hand using fresh fruit, cream, and milk, these frozen treats on a stick are made without preservatives, coloring, or additives. Looking to join the slow food movement and spread its ideals, Denise Drenkelfort and Torsten Alberts teamed up to provide a fresh alternative to industrially made ice cream. Following in the paletas tradition, they make all of their popsicles by hand with fresh regional fruits, vegetables, herbs, and flowers. Their creative flavor combinations include cucumber-lemon-ginger, raspberry-hibiscus, and champagne-strawberry. ◇

How organic soy milk found its way to New York City

Soy Hound's fresh, artisanal soy milk is inspired by the homemade soy milk Nayana Pornchewangkul and Victor Yee remember from their childhoods in Asia. As transplants to New York City, they were disappointed to find only highly processed soy milk in the supermarkets. What began as a personal project to make a high-quality version at home turned into a business specializing in fresh, organic soy milks. Flavors such as Matcha Green Tea, Spicy Ginger, Thai Tea Fusion, and Original are all created with no preservatives. Only organic and non-GMO soybeans, and simple flavorings such as ginger, honey, and raw sugar are used.

Marou, Faiseurs de Chocolat

Organic Vietnamese chocolate reaches world-class level

◇ Marou, Faiseurs de Chocolat has the distinction of producing Vietnam's first single-origin, gourmet chocolate bars. Its practice of using cacao that is grown, fermented, and dried at small farms scattered throughout the southern provinces of Vietnam guarantees the best beans for its fragrant chocolate bars. Marou's founders are two Frenchmen with varied backgrounds: Samuel grew up on a farm in the southwest of France and Vincent has lived all over the world, working in advertising and film. Their shared love for Vietnam and the country's commitment to sharing its wealth amongst its largely rural population made it the perfect location to develop their business, in turn supporting the country they now call home.

Lava Lemonade

The pretty way of making lemonade

The lemonade stand is a classic DIY moment in childhood that designer Ola Mirecka revisited for an installation at London's Royal College of Art. Her LAVA lemonade stand is an interactive space where visitors are invited into an otherworldly environment. Here, they can drink homemade lemonade from handmade glasses while popping lemonade balloons. The handmade signs and community aspect of the project are reminiscent of the resourcefulness and creativity of childhood endeavors, and reflect how those skills are put to good use in later years.

Das Geld hängt an den Bäumen

Money hangs on trees

◇ Bringing together resources that are unused and forgotten in society, the project Money Hangs on Trees takes its name as a motto. The Hamburg-based initiative employs disabled and socially marginalized people to harvest, produce, and sell high-quality apple juice sourced from local apples that would otherwise go to waste. Apples are picked from trees growing on public green areas or in private gardens, or are donated from area farms with surplus stock. The proceeds from the sale of the apple juice, which is produced in a "slow food" cider mill, are then used to pay the wages of the disabled workers. For project founder Jan-Peter Schierhorn, the project translates a humanist, ecological outlook into an economically viable business.

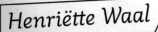

Henriëtte Waal

Meet an outdoor
apple cider brewery

◊ Artist and public space designer
Henriëtte Waal's outdoor apple
cider brewery produces cider
from local apple trees for the
Werkplaats Buijtenland, a project
that also includes a mobile
kitchen and a small bed for overnight guests. As the population
increases in the Dutch countryside, dramatic changes are taking
place in the region's landscape.
Werkplaats Buijtenland works
with designers to develop interactive projects that tie people
to the landscape through shared
experiences, and helps newcom-
ers become aware of their impact
◊ on the rural environment.

A mobile kitchen travels the Dutch countryside

The Dutch landscape is undergoing a transformation as more people move into what were once sparsely populated, agricultural areas. The Werkplaats Buijtenland project looks for ways to positively influence the effect that human activity has on the landscape by making people aware of their surroundings through shared experiences. As part of its initiative, the project asked Studio Elmo Vermijs to design the Buijtenkichten, a mobile kitchen that could be transported to dinners and workshops. Based on the design of a small farm building from the area that had been used to make bread for the surrounding community, the tiny structure is now open for local, regional, and national cooks to learn new ways to prepare and preserve using ingredients from the region.

Rediscovering forgotten food processing techniques

◊ Common objects like flowerpots, pans, tableware, adhesive tape, and chicken wire are the starting points for product designer Casper Tolhuisen's design practice. His work includes a distillery fashioned from a pan and copper water pipes and a smoker made with stacked flowerpots, which recreates the principle of smoking by relying on food processing techniques that have been widely forgotten. His Barbecue Pot is based on the traditional Turkish way of cooking in a Guvec, which can be filled with vegetables, fruits, meat, or fish, and then ◊ sealed with a lemon, an orange, or leek leaves.

Bols & Hansen

Handmade organic marmalade

◊ Spurred by two friends who shared an interest in cooking and eating, the little jam manufacturer Bols & Hansen started its operations in Berlin-Kreuzberg in 2008. Based in a former bakery, Lillevi Hansen and Gabriele Kutzborski design and confect organic seasonal jam creations. Working with loving care and fresh, local ingredients, they continuously expand and refine their broad range of unconventional flavors, having already thought up 50 new recipes. Fully handmade and cooked in small batches of up to 4 kg to retain the pure fruity taste, these fine jams do not need flavor enhancers, artificial colors, preserving agents, or additional sugar.

The Movement Café

Just what the commuter ordered

During the 2012 Olympic games in London, thousands of extra visitors were expected to use the Greenwich DLR station. As part of a larger development of the area, designer Morag Myerscough was commissioned to design a pop-up cafe called The Movement, which would brighten up the area around the station. Conceived as a gateway to the new borough, the cafe served coffee and organic food in addition to offering a repair shop and storage spaces for commuter bicycles. The cafe became a working example of how food-based businesses can function as the cornerstone of a community.

The magic candy factory

◊ It's easy to see that pâtissier Adriano Zumbo loves Willy Wonka when you enter his new retail shop and restaurant in The Star casino in Sydney. First, the two spaces are connected by a dessert train. Second, they are filled with quirky elements like macaron wallpaper that looks so delicious one might be tempted to take just a little lick. The decor reflects the colorful and saccharine substances concocted in the exposed kitchen, where guests see the giant mixers and industrial droppers that reinforce the idea of a production ◊ line within a working factory.

Glazed

Rock 'n' Roll ice cream flavors on the streets of Paris

◊ Started by Henri Guittet, a former strategic consultant who always found ice cream to be boring, Glazed's vintage Citroën Ice Cream Truck sweeps along Paris' alternative neighborhoods, blending the best organic ingredients with a serious dose of rock 'n' roll attitude. With names like Smoke on the Water, Tunnel of Love, and Black Sugar Sex Magic, his homemade ice cream scoops come with a twist. Madagascar vanilla beans are mixed up with hemp seeds, Mara des Bois strawberries are spiced up with Japanese Sanshô berries (peppery and citrusy), oranges are combined with Campari and balsamic reduction, and dark Valrhona chocolate holds hints of wasabi and ginger. These are definitely the hottest ice creams in town.

€uro Bread by Michael Anastassiades

Feeding Europe with the right questions

◊ Confronted by the Euro crisis during a Kopiaste/ Greece is for Lovers event at London Design Festival 2012, designer Michael Anastassiades's response was to create €uro Bread stamps that question the relevance of inter-European solidarity and suggest giving back more. Each stamp is embossed with a ◊ graphic pattern that depicts the configuration of

the European Parliament, an enhanced version of the European Union flag merging with euro-currency, or Ms. Merkel's portrait. Stamped on what the Greeks call Prosphora loaves—bread offerings often baked at home for the Church and shared with the congregation—the breads become edible mediums that intrinsically carry a unique political message.

Papabubble's candy workshop

◇ Papabubble stores use laboratory tools to demonstrate the process of making candy. Designers Yusuke Seki and Jaime Hayon chose to design Papabubble's Yokohama location with details inspired by the unique artisan candy-makers and their experimental nature. In doing so, they recreated Papabubble's iconic glass jars as bespoke pieces crafted by Massimo Lunardon in Venice. These crystal jars set the Yokohama store apart from the other branches and reinforce its commitment to originality. ◇

Meat & Bread

The perfect set of barbecue condiments

◇ Mustard can be a common condiment on the table. Yet there are so many varieties, from traditional English to French Dijon to Bavarian Süßer Senf—mustard is cultural. For Wallpaper*'s 2012 Handmade issue, Vancouver's unparalleled food store Meat & Bread created the perfect set of barbecue condiments. Frankie Harrington and Cord Jarvie (Meat & Bread) teamed up with chef Joe Sartor to specially create three new BBQ condiments: a meat rub with hints of fennel, coriander and star anise, and a red pepper relish and a balsamic onion jam. The creations are packed in a supersized jar designed by local award-winning creative agency Glasfurd & Walker.
◇ Put condiments back onto your kitchen shelf!

RD

& BREAD
S, VINEGAR,
R AND SALT

MEAT &
BREAD MUSTARD

MEAT &
BREAD MUSTARD

Saucy by Nature

Two globetrotting foodies turned condiment artisans

Anyone who has eaten their way through Southeast Asia, India, Nepal, Europe, the Caribbean, South America, and Africa must have a few recipes and stories to share. After traveling the world, travel-obsessed foodies Przemek Adolf and Monika Luczak found themselves in just such a situation. Inspired by the regional cuisines they sampled and the stories of the people they shared meals with, they began to hand-craft small batches of sauces using fruits and vegetables from New York City's Union Square farmers' market. Now their artisan condiments are available for sale, including Cider Braised Onion, Cilantro Lime, and Tomato Apple Chutney.

Bringing winemaking to the living room

◇ The reward for the laborious process of making wine is the gratification that comes from creating a living and breathing thing that is also pleasurable to drink. This fascinating process often takes place outside the home, however, because the equipment is bulky and aesthetically unappealing. Eindhoven-based designer Sabine Marcelis created House Win to give winemaking an audience. This installation, which requires nurturing and care, exists as a calming presence and celebrates the process of winemaking by bringing it into the home.

From low temperature cooking to high-quality eating

There was a time when Jesper Rydahl, ex-Danish businessman turned raw-food expert, lived on pizzas and sodas. But innovators remain innovators. After launching an online social network that became one of Denmark's top 10 largest websites in 2004, he turned his attention to healthy living and opened a democratic raw food take-away restaurant. 42° Raw instantly became a reference in the healthy fast-food world. Invited to stage his cafe inside the Royal Academy's Café space, Rydahl brings sustainable gastronomy to the Mayfair crowd, featuring initial recipes created by two Danish gourmet chefs, Lasse Askov and Bo Lindegaard.

Every item on the menu respects two principles: all ingredients are 100% plant-based and no dishes are cooked above 42°C—the degree above which enzymes are damaged in cooked foods. Beyond smoothies and raw morning cakes, 42° Raw's specialties include Raw Lasagna—marinated zucchini slices layered with sundried tomato sauce, walnuts, parsley pesto, cashew cream, and baby spinach—or the savory Thai Noodles, made with strips of carrot and zucchini in a curry sauce with red chili, ginger, and coconut oil. Craving bread? The 42°Raw sandwich replaces it with delicious rosemary crackers with pumpkin seeds, carrot, and Brazil nuts. Head out to this place to avoid fast food!

Gasoline Alley Coffee

Not just another coffee shop

New York is filled with great coffee shops, yet few manage to combine great location, cleverly designed interiors, and consistency when it comes to quality. Gasoline Alley Coffee was opened in one of Manhattan's narrowest triangular buildings between Houston and Bleecker, holding onto a vestige of 1960s & 70s NoHo architecture, where car mechanics and gas stations were once part of the neighborhood aesthetic. If the interior and steel façades feature industrial-style doors reminiscent of old auto repair shops, it's because founders Neville Ross and Nick Carnevale wanted their coffee joint to feel local, community-based. Both self-proclaimed coffee lovers (Nick's father owns an espresso bar in Italy and might have triggered his passion for good coffee), Ross and Carnevale offer a short selection of blends roasted by the Chicago-based company Intelligentsia, and concentrate on quality—no tall chai slim lattes here—to serve the best coffee, according to seasonality.

ESPRESSO 2.75 ∘ AMERICA

CORTADO 4.00 ∘ MOCHA 4.50 ∘ P

CHAI LATTE 4.50 ∘ HOT CHOCOLA

BAG OF COFFEE

LUXUS

Pärlans Konfektyr

The golden age of candy

The 1930s was the golden age of candy, a time when confectioners made their sweet specialties by hand with local ingredients. Stockholm's Pärlans Konfektyr seeks to recreate this era, serving artisanal caramels, toffee, and fudge amidst an atmosphere of swing music, period furniture, and sassy dames behind the counter. Owner Lisa Ericson is given to constant experimentation with her all-organic sweets, adding crunchy nuts, exotic spices, sweet fruits, berries, and chocolate to create new combinations from fresh, organic ingredients.

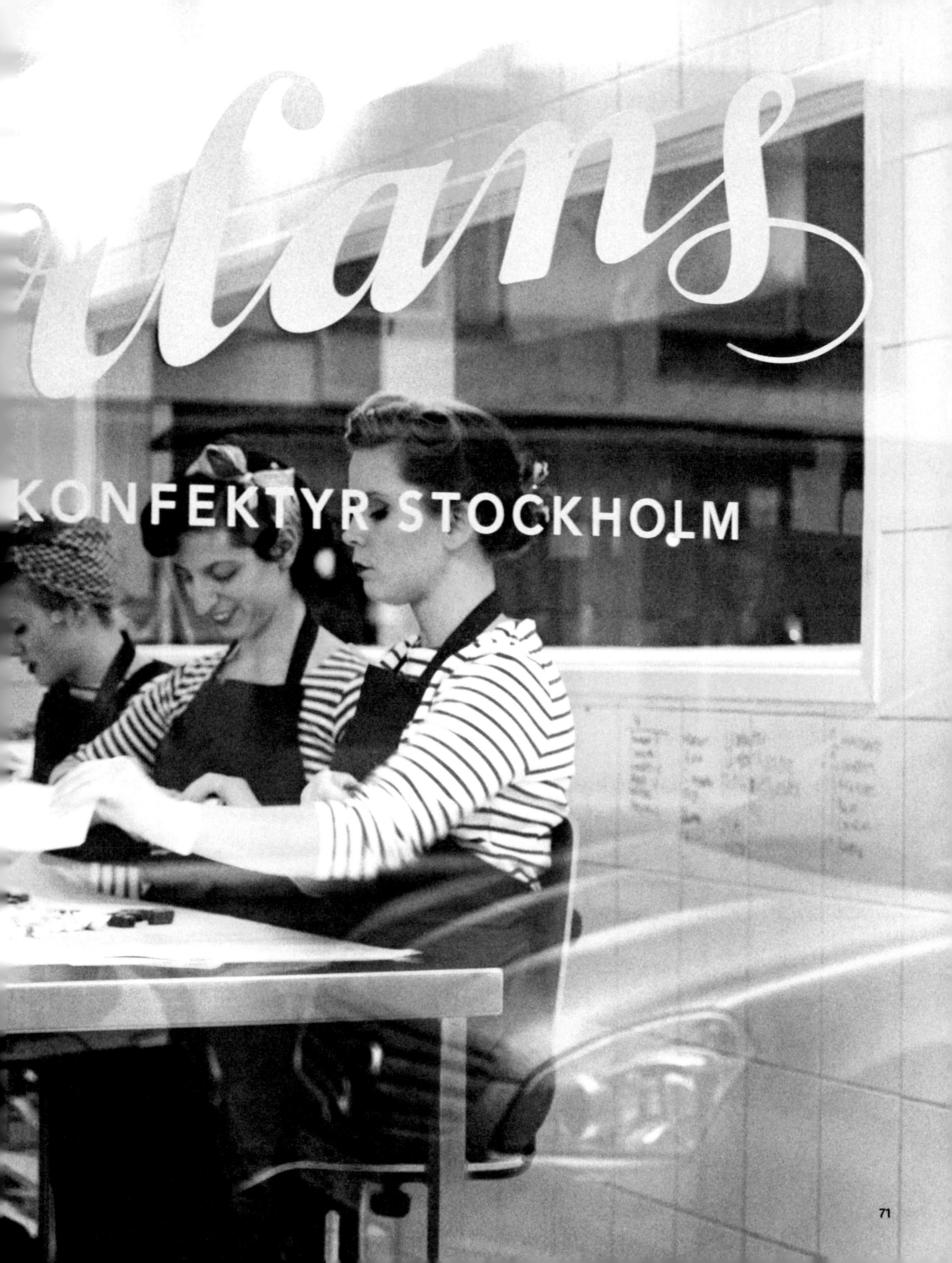
KONFEKTYR STOCKHOLM

The Travelling Gin Co.

They came, they saw, they served

The food truck concept has seeped into the mainstream. But a traveling gin bar on two wheels that comes to you? That is a whole new ballgame. Since 2011, Edward Godden and Joseph Lewis of The Travelling Gin Co. have pedaled their mobile bar to a wide range of venues and locations. Using vintage delivery bicycles, they serve classic gin-based cocktails from baskets and crates that hold ice, limes, local gins, and mixers. This simple setup requires no power, allowing them to easily cater large and small events with no environmental impact. The idea for The Travelling Gin Co. came after Lewis cycled from London to Amsterdam on a vintage butcher bicycle. He fastened a spirit optic to the frame so that he could serve drinks in the evening. The experience was so enjoyable that the idea of a traveling bar soon followed.

Pizza for the people

◇ Del Popolo is a mobile pizzeria committed to creating rustic Neapolitan-inspired pizza using ingredients sourced from small, generational producers around the San Francisco Bay Area. Housed in a 20-foot transatlantic shipping container on wheels, the truck features a wall of glass doors and a traditional wood-fired oven from Italy. Before Del Popolo, Jon Darsky worked at another San Francisco restaurant and noted that other pizzerias in the area either charged outrageous prices for good pizza or low prices for sub-par pies. It was then that he decided to fill in the gap. He began the business in 2010 with a mission to make pizza that is both high-quality and affordable—a decision that is reflected in the name Del Popolo, which means "of the people" in Italian.

Mobile nitro ice cream parlor

◊ Award-winning ice cream entrepreneur Charlie Harry Francis grew up on an ice cream farm in South Wales with his father, an ice cream maker, and his mother, a baker and confectioner. While looking for a way to combine these skills and make delicious custom ice cream creations in front of people's eyes, he founded Lick Me I'm Delicious, the UK's first portable, nitro ice cream parlor. This custom contraption uses a unique liquid nitrogen injection system to create unique and customizable ice cream flavors that are not relegated to the cone, but are allowed to run free and flirt with other ingredients in the cupboard. ◊

The Bitter Truth | PROFILE

Classic cocktails are based on legendary bitters

Some products are all about revisiting the past, sometimes even coloring its picture-perfect postcard memory. The rush for made-to-measure cocktails and crafted spirits has led The Bitter Truth—started by Munich bartenders Stephan Berg and Alexander Hauck when they found it hard to source great cocktail bitters—to emerge as the specialist of old-time bitters.

Let's go back a few centuries. With origins dating back to nearly 300 BC, bitters are the natural heirs to elixirs used to cure everything from tapeworm to high blood pressure. The ancient civilizations of China and Egypt created rudimentary wines from macerated herbs to serve as panaceas along the ancient Silk Route. The shift of these elixirs from medicinal to recreational occurred during the Renaissance under Catherine de Medici when she brought recipes for cordiali along with her Tuscan court. For centuries, each bitter had a unique formula which most Italian families kept strictly secret—a principle still true today. Using herbal, and sometimes suspect ingredients like quinine, ginseng, licorice, or wormwood, cocktail bitters were always the ingredient that distinguished cocktails from other categories of beverages such as Toddies, Slings, Fizzes, Sours, or Punches. In a word, they were, for decades, an essential component of good cocktail creations, before fancy, sweet, and brightly colored cocktails doomed their fate.

But good classic recipes are finally back in trend. "The time for amari—translated from Italian as bitters in the United States—may never be better," writes Jod Kaftan in the LA Times Magazine. "Thanks to the craft-cocktail movement, we've begun trading in our Fuzzy Navels and Cosmos for Manhattans and Highballs. Tacky clubs with velvet ropes are being replaced with rum bars and speakeasies. After decades of cocktails punked with high fructose corn syrup and artificial flavors, we have finally broadened our palate, returning to our classic cocktail pedigree—all things vintage are synonymous with authenticity."

Started in 2006, the German bitters company The Bitter Truth revived classic mixologist craft, thanks to the genuine passion of bartenders Stephan Berg and Alexander Hauck. Both of them had already gained a considerable amount of experience in producing handmade cocktail bitters for the bars they were working at, and Berg owned a large collection of current and historical bitters, some of which hadn't been produced for decades. Digging into old cocktail recipes, it didn't take them long to understand that unless they used the same exact bitter they wouldn't get anywhere near the original taste. Having the correct bitter handy was crucial to revisiting old-time favorites. Spending long hours testing and tasting bitters, they finally started releasing authentically crafted bitters. First came an Orange Bitters and Old Time Aromatic Bitters, followed by a Lemon Bitters, the Jerry Thomas' Own Decanter Bitters, Creole Bitters, and a Celery Bitters. Season after season, they won an impressive series of awards, from "Best Spirit of the Year,"

to "Gold Medal," "Best in Class," and "Best New Product." These accolades came from some of the industry's most prestigious events like Tales of the Cocktail, held in New Orleans each year. This brings us back to world classics and Planters House in St. Louis, where professor and one of the most important bartenders of the nineteenth century, Jerry Thomas (1830–1885), crafted some of the century's best cocktails. Paying tribute to the old man's legacy and his master skills at both the Planters House and New York's Metropolitan Hotel, the Jerry Thomas' Own Decanter Bitters is based on the original recipe used by the professor. "Very fruity and very bitter, it blends citrus and dried fruit aromas with the spicy and

bitter flavors of cloves, angostura bark, and cinnamon. Celery Bitters, also traditionally used in the nineteenth century, became another lost ingredient. Whipped off the best cocktail menus, the product had been extinct for decades. With strong flavors of celery followed by lemongrass, orange peel, and ginger, the bitters were always a cornerstone in crafting traditional corpse-reviver cocktails such as the Bloody Mary, Bullshot, and Prairie Oyster, as well as Martini Cocktails and the famous Gin & Tonic. A critic recently wrote about The Bitter Truth's original Celery Bitters: "The vegetal quality these bitters add to cocktails is quite unique. They're another shining example of a cocktail's past molding its future."

Boys Beer

Time to brew

◊ La Bolleur creates multidisciplinary get-togethers and diverse creative projects that speak to and connect a broad range of people. It is along these lines that brewing beer has always been on top of the studio's to-do-list. The idea took shape at the cultural event Huttenfestival in Tilburg, the Netherlands, where the team installed a tap installation with a beer tower, an ice tunnel, and a bar. To round off their vision of creating the best beer experience, they teamed up with a small organic brewery to develop their own beer brand. Boys Bier was first brought into action at a party series during Dutch Design Week, which La Bolleur preferred to call Deutsche Design Woche, better suited to the occasion in ironically responding to what they considered the event's "anti-foreign design policy."

Put A Egg On It

Biannual magazine about the joy of eating together

◊ Put A Egg On It is an irreverent, digest-sized art and literary magazine about food, cooking, and the communal joys of eating with friends and family. Published biannually on green paper in Brooklyn, it features personal stories, illustrations, photo essays of dinner parties and special art projects, and practical cooking tips and recipes. Each issue of Put A Egg On It includes a selection of regionally packaged foods accompanied by the personal perspective of someone who grew up with them. These products, which have survived and thrived in local areas despite the growth of corporate food production, highlight the importance of diversity in regional foods and brands.

PUT
A
EGG
ON IT

$7.00US

0 74470 26491 0   06>

TASTY ZINE #6

PUT
A
EGG
ON IT

Tasty Zine #4 $7

$7.00US

0 74470 26491 0   04>

VL92 Gin

The heritage gin

◇ When Dutch entrepreneurs Sietze Kalkwijk and Rick de Zwart succeeded in creating their version of the ultimate gin, its recipe and brand were built on the Jenever tradition of the Netherlands. It was the Dutch who first shipped this herbal-flavored liquor from the Netherlands to the United Kingdom in the early seventeenth century. Four hundred years later, VL92 Gin was named after a historic Dutch sailing ship whose cargo included exotic spices perfect for VL92, which derives its complexity from botanical elements that finish with a citrusy endnote of coriander leaf. To continue the tradition, the first shipment of VL92 Gin distributed outside the Netherlands was delivered to London on May 15, 2012 by a ship that originated in Vlaardingen, Netherlands.

961 Beer

War journalist turned brewmaster
teaches Lebanese about quality

◊ It all started in 2006 during the war and the darkest days of the Lebanese people. Tired of the lack of quality beer in Lebanon, ex-war reporter Mazen Hajjar and his friends started to brew beer in his kitchen, 20 liters at a time. While war and blockades are not the ideal conditions under which to start a company, they went ahead with it anyway, despite everyone telling them they were crazy to even consider it. Quickly, 961 went from being the smallest brewery in the world, and the only microbrewery in the Middle East (which it still is), to brewing nearly 2 million liters per year. Today, 961 Beer comprises four regular beers—Lager, Porter, Red Ale, Witbier—along with other seasonal flavors and a Brewmaster's Select called Lebanese Pale Ale. One thing hasn't changed since the first day of Hajjar's company. He has stuck to the exact same founding principles of using only traditional techniques, quality ingredients, and putting lots of love in every pint they craft.

Juice Press

The luxury of uncompromised organic juices

After selling luxury goods as part of a decades-long family business that dealt in art, antiques, and jewelry, co-founder Marcus Antebi started Juice Press out of a love for healthy food—real healthy food—as in "uncompromised, organic, and well-prepared." Raw food-adept, and processed food's worst enemy, Marcus Antebi is definitely a purist. Juice Press was created in his image, as a company that sells a selection of all-organic cold-pressed juices, plus packaged foods created by Jermaine Jonas, a chef known for his vegan touch. Jonas is behind the success of restaurant Pure Food and Wine. Embark on a curative, detox journey with Dr. Green Juice, a mix of kale, pineapple, apple, lemon, and ginger, or order a serving of The Guru, a superfood smoothie that is a dietician's dream with its super-nutritious content of coconut water and coconut meat, whole-blended apple, vegan DHA omega oil, goji berries, banana, blueberry, hemp protein powder, hemps seeds, and raw cacao. Trust its content, not its color!

Fernando Laposse

Lolly poppers

Product designer Fernando Laposse started using sugar as a design material when he decided to replicate the art of glass blowing in a domestic environment. What started as an experiment soon became well-known performances that use rotational molding to produce drinking glasses out of melted sugar. The glasses are then consumed by the guests, who use them to swirl their beverages, which causes the piece to slowly dissolve and the contents to become progressively sweeter. Once the drink is consumed, the glass becomes a kind of lollipop. French-born and Mexico-raised Laposse considers himself a product designer and not a chef, although he welcomes the overlap that his practice has made with food, which he sees as the ultimate DIY expression of creativity.

Brooklyn BrewShop

The do-it-yourself set for upcoming brewmasters

◇ Erica Shea and Stephen Valand started the Brooklyn Brew Shop to reintroduce consumers to the pleasures of homemade beer. Their philosophy is based on the belief that fresh, whole ingredients combined with traditional recipes make it possible for anyone to brew delicious beer. With flavors such as Bruxelles Black Beer, Chestnut Brown Ale, Chocolate Maple Porter, and Jalapeño Saison, each of their stylish and playful brewing kits emphasizes the fun side of brewing beer and are designed especially for stove-top brewing. ◇

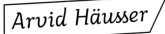

Arvid Häusser

Rediscovering the coffee-making experience

◇ Arvid Häusser designed the innovative Seppl espresso
maker while he was still a student at the Bauhaus
University in Weimar, Germany. Created in partner-
ship with the KAHLA porcelain company, this wall-
mounted porcelain espresso maker saves counter
space and simplifies the coffee-making experience
by exposing each of the machine's individual components. The Seppl's separate parts, which are made
from recyclable materials, can be stacked together
◇ for easy loading into the dishwasher.

Quinn Popcorn

The time was right to reinvent microwave popcorn

◊ As self-proclaimed non-activists who don't always eat the right food all the time, Coulter and Kristy Lewis nevertheless wanted a healthier, sustainably produced snack food. It was the birth of their son Quinn that pushed them to make a better microwave popcorn that they could feel good about feeding to him. They replaced the traditional chemical-coated bags with compostable paper bags and filled them with flavored organic popcorn made without preservatives or GMO ingredients. Microwavable Quinn Popcorn comes in unusual but tempting flavors such as parmesan and rosemary or lemon and sea salt.

Nong's Khao Man Gai

One simple dish, prepared to perfection

◇ Thai Nong only serves one dish in her tiny Portland-based food truck. It is one that looks deceptively simple at first sight: some rice, a steamed chicken breast, a cup of clear broth, some sauce, fresh cilantro, and a few cucumber slices, all wrapped in a paper foil. Brought up in Thailand, Nong knows, however, that Khao Man Gai—chicken over rice—is one of those foods, that when made to perfection, is the essence of comfort food. Food for the Gods, some even say. Nong doesn't take any shortcuts for a meal she sells at $6.75. Instead, she stays true to her Thai roots and keeps her dish authentic with only the best, hand-selected ingredients. Some may say that it's pretty bold to open a food cart with only one dish, but this has paved her way to success. Already, Nong runs two ad-
◇ ditional locations, including one at the local university.

Bon Chovie

The way to someone else's heart is through his or her stomach

◊ When a chick from Seattle with a metal head and a green thumb marries a charter boat captain and all-around seafood maniac from Florida's Gulf Coast, you get the Brooklyn-based Bon Chovie. Cooking side by side, Renae and Neill Holland use a non-traditional approach to food to create signature dishes like anchovy filets cured in white wine vinegar on diced tomato and toast with a dusting of smoked paprika, or fried anchovies one of two ways: "Jersey Style" (head-on preparation) or "The Original" (heads removed).

Ovenly

Brooklyn's local snack supplier

◇ Agatha Kulaga and Erin Patinkin originally met at
a book club that encouraged members to contribute a
food dish to each meeting. Recognizing their shared
love of cooking and baking, the two soon decided
to go professional, turning what had been a hobby
into a business that supplies bars and coffee shops
with sweet and salty snack foods. Due to a diverse
client base, their offerings range from pastries
and cookies to nuts and popcorn. Their Maple Thyme
Pecans make a perfect pairing with hoppy beers,
cocktails, or wine, while the Spicy Bacon Caramel
Corn is made with organic popcorn and bacon.

Rick's Picks

Food entrepreneur starts with childhood memories

◇ Rick's Picks founder, Rick Field, grew up making traditional pickles with his family in the Vermont countryside. After moving to New York City to pursue a career in television production, he missed his family's summer ritual and decided to recreate it. His passion for pickling turned into the driving force behind Rick's Picks, which are distinguished by their exceptional quality and an unusual array of varieties and flavors, including Windy City Wasabeans and Smokra. His 14 varieties of shelf-stable pickles are hand-packed and made in season with produce from local farmers. ◇

Chickpea and Olive

Vegan street food

◇ It was the adoption of a strict vegetarian diet that transformed chef Daniel Strong's approach to food. His new perspective resulted in a commitment to ensuring that no flavor becomes muted and that every ingredient is used with purpose. After working in kitchens all over Manhattan and as sous chef at an Italian trattoria, he opened Chickpea and Olive with food lover Danielle Ricciardi. It is here that they combine their passion for food to create vegan fare that is prepared with organic ingredients. Their menus are designed with a less-is-more philosophy to showcase the stars of the show: fruits and vegetables grown on small, ◇ local farms.

Pizza Pilgrims

Where Italians eat their pizza when in London

Here comes another clever food truck, closer to a Vespa than an actual truck. Built into the back of a Piaggo Ape, Pizza Pilgrims serves Napoli-inspired street food from the back of its wood-fired oven. The Ape was first used by brothers James & Thom Elliot to drive around Italy while they learned how to make the perfect Neapolitan pizza after both quitting their jobs. The Ape is now parked in London's Berwick Street Market during the day, and on a new rooftop supper club on Brick Lane, Forza Win, in the evenings. In just a few months, their mouth-watering pizzas have gained a solid reputation and the brothers are now known as the "best non-Italian pizza-makers in town." Expect to see true Italians at heart stalling outside the shack for a great pizza.

Tacombi

First we take Manhattan…

With vintage graphics and sun-drenched colors, Tacombi's visual identity evokes, in itself, a trip to beachside Yucatan. And that was precisely the idea behind it when Monterrey-born chef Dario Wolos teamed up with Food Network chef Aaron Sanchez to take New York's taco tradition to the next level. Now parked in a concrete garage just off Houston Street, the once nomad 1963 Volkswagen van pops open to welcome a funky, open-air kitchen that serves typical Mexican fare. Order from a long list of tacos and quesadillas, fill your glass with horchata and hibiscus juice, and take a seat at one of the hand-painted folding tables or counters scattered around. You'll feel Mexico's vibrant bohemian atmosphere light up your lunch break, without moving.

London Fields Brewery

Craft the draft

◊ One of the most culturally vibrant areas of London
is the borough of Hackney. But somehow, amidst its
growing culture of locally handcrafted products, not
a brewery was to be found. The folks behind London
Fields Brewery decided to right that wrong when
they opened their brewery in 2011. Located under the
railway arches, next to the oasis of greenery that
is London Fields, it is just one of a growing number
of London breweries helping to spread the word of
craft beer around the country, and put Hackney on
◊ the map as a destination for great beer.

The local soul
of organic spirits

◇ Bill Welter opened an organic
distillery in the midwestern
United States as a way to
support the local organic farming
movement while encouraging
others to invest in the land and
its people. Welter began work
on Journeyman Distillery by
renovating an old factory building with repurposed materials
from his family's farm in Indiana.
The distillery now produces
certified organic spirits with
unique, subtle flavors in small,
handcrafted batches. This
drinking experience helps support small farms in a variety
◇ of sustainable ways.

The chef-thinker, popularizing simple ideas that upend the way people think about the food we eat

Imagine a farm, a proper 80-acre farm just 25 miles (or 35 minutes) from Manhattan. Dream or reality? Reality. Established on a former Rockefeller estate, Stone Barns Center for Food & Agriculture is a working farm and education center dedicated to training aspiring farmers and raising public awareness of resilient farming. Run as a non-profit organization, the center also welcomes 10,000 children raised in intense urban environments every year through school trips, and another 100,000 gastronomes and locals who venture out for fresh air and locally grown food. Miles away from a 30-million-person megalopolis, Stone Barns Center is dedicated to sharing knowledge about the soil and the environment around it. Students are shown how to pick vegetables while cooking and gardening classes are organized for adults and families.

In 2011, the Growing Farmers Initiative was launched. The Initiative, which includes farm apprenticeships, technical workshops, an annual conference, and the online hub VirtualGrange.org, targets a hybrid generation of young professionals, most with a degree in hand, who would rather work in contact with the land than in the stressful environment of urban jobs. Think accountants who would rather be farmers on the plains. On site, they are taught how to compost, rear pigs outdoors, landscape, and even repair mechanical tools. The beginning farmers' curriculum also covers marketing, business planning and food policy—all part of learning about a way of farming that combines agricultural tradition (heritage breed Bourbon Red turkeys) with innovative experimentation (non-GMO hybrid vegetable varieties, bred for exceptional flavor).

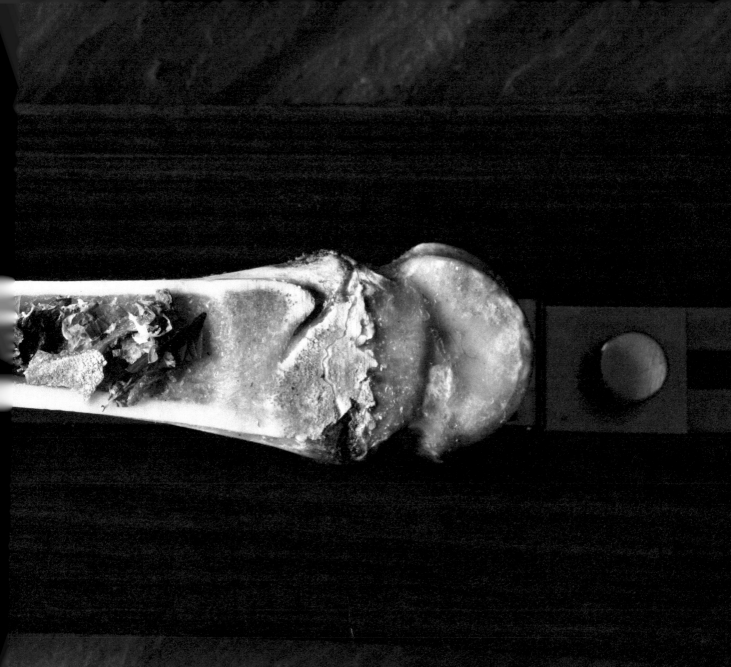

And behind this exemplary initiative and well-run new-generation farm hides another kind of experiment: the restaurant Blue Hill at Stone Barns and the cuisine of executive chef and co-owner Dan Barber, whose dedication to seasonal, locally sourced food has put him at the forefront of American gastronomy. "Dan Barber practices a kind of close-to-the-land cooking married to agriculture and stewardship of the earth," explains his TED-talk profile. At the height of the growing season up to 80% of what Barber serves at Blue Hill at Stone Barnes comes directly from the property Blue Hill Farm in Great Barrington, Massachusetts, and from a variety of other local farms. He is known for being a think tank of his own. Invited to speak at a TED conference, Dan Barber squared off with a dilemma that faces many chefs today: how to keep fish

on the menu. Over the first few minutes of the talk, he crusaded against the evolving nature of the fish we are served. "For the past 50 years, we've been fishing the seas like we clear-cut forests. It's hard to overstate the destruction. 90% of large fish, the ones we love—the tunas, the halibuts, the salmons, swordfish—they've collapsed. They are now the intensively fish-farmed leading and fed with chicken flours." And what is sustainable about feeding chicken to fish? That is precisely his concern. Uncompromising, Dan Barber preaches for a radically new concept of agriculture, one in which the food actually tastes good! According to him, mentalities need to change, as foodies are always seen as a bit too radical, as passionate lovers rather than realists who cherish farmers' markets and family farms, and eat local and organic.

"Even if we are seen as dreamers, we foodies ensure the future of good food; we challenge our habits and are open to new taste. But more important, we are not open to any sort of compromise when our health and the future of taste are at stake," Dan Barber likes to repeat.

More recently, Chef Barber stressed the way in which the modern world is invaded by low-quality wheat and flours, and how a truly viable food system must grow its own grain. "It all comes down to grain," says Barber. "First, because it's delicious—a whole world of flavors that's been ignored for the past 50 years—but also because it's a critical missing link in any community's ability to feed itself." As an example, he talks about how New York was the region's breadbasket back in the eighteenth century, producing wheat for consumption there and in neighboring states. But as canal and railroad systems allowed for long-distance transport, cheap grain rolled in from the large, flat farms in the Midwest, and the small community mills dotting the Hudson Valley crumbled. Today, some farmers are working to rebuild the Empire State's grain industry, following the lead of farmers resurrecting local grain economies across the country, from New Mexico to Pennsylvania. Once again, Dan Barber stresses the importance of plunging back into history to reinvent the future of food, to push for a renaissance of extinct practices that are still viable. In short, we need to be attentive and intelligent about all things we eat, and look both forward and back to grow our own food with dedication.

Orange Olive

Experiencing pure food at its origin

Djoeke Delnooz founded his catering business, Orange Olive, on a commitment to using only pure ingredients that are respectful to people, animals, and the environment. Working with design agency Silo, he developed a brand that communicates this fresh and natural approach to food, including Orange Olive's Puur Smaak Diners (Pure Taste Dinners). These unique dining experiences bring consumers closer to the origin of flavorful ingredients through on-site dinners in locations such as the Hoeve Biesland cow and sheep farm, the Scheveningen fish auction, and the Westland strawberry greenhouse. Each meal is prepared by Michelin star chefs including Niven Kunz, Jef Schuur, and Edwin Vinke, and is served at long dining tables where participants are surrounded by interesting conversation and the source of their food.

Kääntöpöyta

Urban farm on Finnish tracks

◇ An abandoned area of Helsinki's Pasila district was a no man's land before the environmental NGO Dodo revitalized it in 2009. It began with an urban farming movement that transformed the location into Turntable, an urban garden, cafe, greenhouse, and public space. Situated in Pasila's historic railway yard, the project became an urban farming test lab and a source of learning and inspiration. In addition to offering various workshops, events, and locally grown food in the Turntable cafe, the garden also has a beehive, dry toilet, composts, cob oven, and solar panels to produce energy.

Farm London

Inner-city growth

There is a storefront in central London where food lovers and urban farmers can meet for a cup of coffee and to smell the countryside. FARM:shop is a functioning farm packed to the rafters with plants, an aquaponic micro fish farming system, a polytunnel, and a rooftop chicken coop. The enterprise, also home to a workspace, cafe, and events venue, was started by Something & Son, an eco-social design practice, as part of a larger FARM: project that aims to bring farming to the city by developing a network of shops and grow sites across the UK.

Oatmeal Studio

The hanging gardens of The Hague

Some of the best moments of summer are outdoor meals eaten under a canopy of trees. When Filmhuis den Haag asked Oatmeal Studio to create an architectonic interference for their summer restaurant, the Dutch collective decided to make a hanging vegetable garden inspired by both summer memories and one of the Seven Wonders of the World. Their connection between production and consumption gave guests a new eating experience; with a view of The Hague's skyline, guests were surrounded by a hanging garden of zucchini, tomato, strawberry, and gooseberry plants, as well as fig and apple trees and a wide assortment of herbs. During their meal, diners were invited to enrich their food with fresh herbs or just pick a nearby strawberry.

Heading out, slowing down

◇ The Agrarian Kitchen is, by definition, related to land. So it comes naturally that this cooking school is committed to reconnecting the kitchen with the land, a place where one rediscovers the simple pleasures of gathering and cooking with produce in close contact with the soil. This adventure is led by Rodney Dunn and his wife Séverine Demanet, a young couple who wanted to free themselves from urban constraints and reconnect with the source. Set on five acres, their agrarian farm houses a vegetable garden, an orchard, a berry patch, and an herb garden, all grown using organic principles. Also in residence are Wessex Saddleback pigs, Barnevelder chickens, two British Alpine goats, and a flock of geese, Rodney Dunn proudly explains, leaving out that he also ventures into growing amazing herbs such as wasabi leaf ("use like celery") or goat's rue and sweet cicely ("perfect with rhubarb"), bringing out the former chef in him. "The fresh herbs are growing out of hand, the zucchini flowers are in bloom, the radishes are incredibly sweet this year, and there's enough lettuce to feed a whole village." Daily life at the farm comes with endless surprises in what nature can produce, and sometimes multiply.

That is precisely what prompted ex-full-time food editor of Gourmet Traveller Rodney Dunn and his wife Séverine Demanet to flee Sydney and settle in a nineteenth-century schoolhouse 45 minutes north of Hobart, Tasmania.

"I wanted to have access to better food," he tells writer and colleague Pat Nourse. "I really wanted to eat vegetables we couldn't buy, to live the experience of having one's own animals and milk. And almost as important, to make a living out of sharing that experience with other people." ◇

From the start, there was no room for compromise. "The core of our philosophy is to rely solely on sustainable farming practices and introduce as few outside inputs as possible. The name of our farm also suggests recreating the agrarian system that predated the industrial revolution: a subsistence farming system where farmers grew a range of food crops and had animals that complemented each other to provide food for their families and local community. The gardens were then looked after using organic principles (no chemicals or artificial fertilizers), and, back in the day, they grew so many heirloom varieties that vegetable gardens were a paradise for diversity."

Once the farm was set up, Dunn and Demanet launched Tasmania's first hands-on, farm-based cooking school. Focusing on agrarian lifestyle (during which one forages the ripest vegetables before cooking them), artisanal subjects (such as making cheese and butter, preserving, baking bread, making pasta, charcuterie, ice-cream, and confections), or paddock-to-plate experiences for children, the three types of cooking classes cater to different needs, all of which loop back to raising awareness about sustainable living and self-empowerment. As much as it might seem like a gamble to leave a job in the city to turn a schoolhouse into a working farm, Dunn and Demanet are there to show that it is not only possible, but a life-changing experience. Their choice actually tells a lot about a new generation of self-taught entrepreneurs who look at farms like the new lifestyle frontier as a place where they can sculpt a life of their own. Spreading across the globe, the examples of places and people involved in this movement are numerous, from South African lifestyle farm and haven Babylonstoren, which welcomes children from Cape Town and style gurus on the lookout for a clean weekend, to chefs like Paul Cunningham, who left stellar restaurant Tivoli to take over Henne Kirkeby Farm (established in 1790) in the Danish countryside, growing his own herbs and vegetables and shaping the future of Nordic cuisine.

As much as these kinds of rural journeys seem solitary, they are all about reconnecting with the land and the locals that bear the memory of the land. No charcuterie class at The Agrarian Kitchen comes without the skills of local butcher and pig breeder Lee Christmas, who lends a hand with the Whole Hog class. Baker Graham Prichard also brings his passion for wood-fired sourdough, while another imported character, Rainer Oberle, a trained horticulturist and former head gardener in German research and botanical gardens, teaches gardening workshops. And so this sustainable Tasmanian cooking school brings us back to the soil, the roots, and the plants—back to the basics.

Morris Kitchen

Building a business from a holiday memory

The story started in the South of France around a simple bottle of ginger syrup. From then on, sister-and-brother team Kari and Tyler Morris took flavoring syrups to a new level. She had come to New York to organize art fairs; he had been cooking in restaurants for 13 years. Using pure freshly grated ginger juice and sugar, they first reproduced the original syrup before crafting variations such as Preserved Lemon, Spiced Apple (which uses apples from a New York State farm, blended with cinnamon and star anise) and Rhubarb, the company's seasonal summer syrup. Bottled in signature amber glass containers, and wrapped in a letterpress label that is hand-stamped with the batch number, they perfectly embody Brooklyn's surge of locally crafted artisan products.

Hot Rum Cow

High octane publication

◇ Great beers, wines, and spirits have extraordinary stories and people behind their delicious flavors. But publisher Fraser Allen noticed that in a world of food magazines, there were no beautifully designed drink magazines that told interesting stories. In 2012 he changed this with Hot Rum Cow, a quarterly print magazine designed for people who are curious about what they drink. Like the independent breweries, boutique distilleries, and specialty suppliers that it covers, the publication, which has a growing fan base, keeps its operation small with an emphasis on quality.

Société-Orignal

Handmade and hand-delivered to chefs and connoisseurs

One doesn't come across terms like "Boreal Agriculture" and "Gastronomic Agriculture" every day. What do they mean? An oddball, Montreal-based culinary company Société-Orignal works as a dedicated, ethical grocery that teams up with farmers and foragers across rural Québec to uncover new culinary products, distributing them mostly to chefs and acclaimed restaurateurs across North America. Deliberately targeting a niche clientele of experts and connoisseurs, Société-Orignal explains that they can only offer limited editions because they work with real farmers and never try to push nature's limits. For example, unusual herbs and spices are foraged, while sunflower oil and maple syrup bottles are limited to the harvests of individual farmers. When Société-Orignal hand-delivers to the best restaurants in Toronto or New York, the products come in clear glass jars containing intriguing edibles: green alder cones (similar to long pepper); myrica gale spike (like pistachio-colored dried mulberries with sharp points); cow parsnip seeds; young juniper berries soaked in vinegar-like capers; or Gaspésie maritime honey. Cutting-edge and conscientious, gastronomic agriculture is exemplified.

The ice cream exploration kit

◇ The Ice Cream Concept Parlour uses the process of making ice cream to explore connections between food and design. It also encourages users to appreciate and connect with the process of making what they eat. Its creator, Ploenpit Nittaramorn, has a background in design research as well as product and graphic design. She takes a narrative and experimental approach to her work, which is focused on finding new ways to experience food. She believes that industrial food preparation and packaging, which allow consumers to purchase ready-made meals and pre-cut products, has weakened the relationship between people and their food. Her work aims to remind consumers of where food comes from, while rekindling ◇ their appreciation for the cooking process.

Kokako

Auckland's first organic roastery

When Mike Murphy acquired an old post office building in Auckland, he set out to convert the space into an organic roastery and cafe that reflected his commitment to sustainability. Working together with designer Chris Stevens, they transformed the space using interior elements found at a local demolition yard, including doors and windows from houses in the neighborhood and light fixtures from another defunct local post office. As Auckland's first organic roastery, Kokako promotes ethical trading with Fairtrade growers and funds environmental initiatives such as the rehabilitation of New Zealand's endangered Kokako bird.

Restaurant Day

Anyone can open a restaurant anywhere— for one day

◇ In Helsinki, where food trucks are prohibited, many up-and-coming food entrepreneurs never have the chance to try out new ideas. In response to these stifling laws, Timo Santala founded Restaurant Day, a day of pop-up restaurants, cafes, and bars in a city where many people are eager to try new and experimental foods. The event, which started with just 40 participants in its first year, encourages participants to use a wide variety of locations including homes, offices, street corners, courtyards, parks, and the beach. By its second year, Restaurant Day had grown to 680 restaurants in multiple countries, offering a diverse selection of foods including a boiled bagel stand, fresh blinis served with smoked salmon and cream cheese, Mediterranean muffins, and grilled hamburgers.

Setting the stage for unique food experiences

◊ An exploding cake, an audio feed from a pile of bones, and an espresso sponge also known as modernist coffee. These are just some of the projects that food designers Blanch & Shock have created together with artists, producers, scientists, and chefs. Using carefully sourced seasonal British ingredients, their work provides opulent food with a minimum of waste for pop-up dinners, edible installations, performances, and lectures. Inspired by the technology of modern cookery, their work focuses on sustainability, ◊ history, and the psychology of eating.

Mobile Gastfreundschaft (Mobile Hospitality Project)

Meeting a stranger over food and drinks can be the starting point for great conversations and relationships. The Mobile Gastfreundschaft project, from designers Ania Rosinke and Maciej Chmara, brings a mobile kitchen into the outdoors, inviting passersby to the table for food and conversation. Made entirely out of wood, the kitchen has a welcoming DIY-aesthetic that communicates the warmth and joy of food culture. The pair, who originally met at the Academy of Fine Arts in Gdańsk, Poland, now live and work in Vienna, Austria. Social responsibility and interaction with public space are important components of their architecture and design practice, which combines craftsmanship with a conceptual and ecological approach.

The Social Act

Copenhagen's bi-monthly comfort food experience

In Copenhagen, Bo Lindegaard and Lasse Askov are true odd-balls. Since meeting in culinary school, where they admit to having initially hated each other, they've worked on diverse food-related projects under the banner of I'm a Kombo, bringing outrageous creativity to the catering world. Launched in spring 2012, The Social Act logically pushes their vision to a more community-based audience. Less pop-up and more part-time restaurant, The Social Act acts as a platform for performance. Every two months, Lindegaard and Askov host a handful of dinner parties for a 14-person guest list. The menu is composed of nine perfectly crafted dishes gathered around all of their food values—contrast, interaction, form, function, trend, innovation, and surprise—which are all used to highlight "comfort food," the concept's central pillar. A new dining experience is born.

Fuchsia Flower Grocery

Baking with edible flowers

◊ Flowers are more than just decorations for Binky Holleran, chef and owner of Fuchsia Epicerie Fleur, a small artisan grocery shop in Montreal. Her store specializes in products made with edible flowers such as the Floral Cookie Jar, which contains a simple cookie mix for delicious, floral-flavored cookies made with top-quality, healthy ingredients. Her floral extract packets contain concentrated floral extracts for use in baking and cooking. Each packet is designed to elevate the experience of even the most ordinary puddings, cakes, or whipped cream
◊ with floral scents and flavors.

Xocolatl de David

Sweet & Spicy

After growing up between the United States, Australia, and Singapore, David Briggs developed adventurous tastes in food that reflect the regional cuisines of his youth. As an adult, Briggs became a professional chef in Portland, Oregon, and eventually began experimenting with chocolate. Soon after, he found himself crafting chocolates and confections full time. In keeping with the experimental flavors of his childhood, the products from Xocolatl de David lean more toward the savory than the sweet, with intriguing flavors such as Bacon Caramel, Sourdough and Olive Oil, or Foie Gras.

Pot + Pantry

San Francisco's kitchenware boutique

It was a plate of tomatoes and fresh mozzarella that made Donna Suh Wageman a lover of simple, locally harvested food. Pot + Pantry, her small kitchen boutique in San Francisco's Mission neighborhood, is an extension of this love and a way to bring food lovers together with new and gently used kitchenware. Like stepping into a friend's kitchen, her shop feels personal because she stocks only items that she knows, uses, and loves. The inventory reflects her shopping philosophy, which places value on buying classic, well-made products that will last a long time. Getting to know her clients and the items they buy and sell in her shop allows her to share the story behind each piece and pass it on to its new owner.

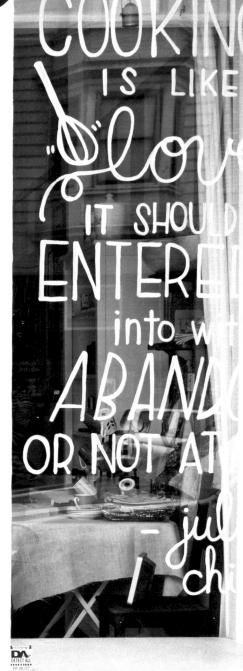

t & pantry

593

pot & pantry
OPEN

COOKING
IS LIKE
"love"
IT SHOULD BE
ENTERED
into with
ABANDON
OR NOT AT ALL

— julia
child

Haven's Kitchen

New York's casual meeting place for foodies

◊ Just two blocks from New York City's Union Square Greenmarket, there is
a haven for the food community. Located in a cozy carriage house, Havens
Kitchen is a recreational cooking school, a specialty food shop, and an
event space dedicated to the preparation and enjoyment of delicious,
sustainable, and seasonal food. It was while working on her Masters in
Food Studies in 2010 that Alison Schneider imagined a place where people
could come together to learn and teach each other about food in a way
that benefits the environment and the local economy. Havens Kitchen
uses education to increase demand for locally and sustainably produced
products, and contributes to helping small and mid-sized farmers make
◊ a good living, grow more food, and feed more people.

Cemilzade Confiserie Orientale

Turkish delight since 1883

The Cemilzade Confiserie Orientale is a traditional Turkish confectionary that produces handmade marzipan, lo-kums (also known as Turkish Delight), and candies from secret family recipes that use all natural ingredients. Founded in 1883 in Istanbul by Udi Cemil Bey, it is still owned and operated by the Cemilzade family, who maintain the tradition of making sweets that are fresh and light. The interior of the Berlin location, with its white furniture, velvet cushions, and gold-leaf walls, recalls the Oriental interiors of the early twentieth century, and reinforces the confectionary's standing as a leader in quality Turkish sweets.

Télescope Cafe

Saving Paris

◇ Coffee lovers in Paris have long bemoaned the city's lack of good coffee. In the short time since it opened in 2012, Télescope Cafe has become beloved to locals and tourists alike as the place to go for an excellent coffee. Owners Nicolas Clerc and David Flynn are experienced baristas who roast their own beans and personally prepare each cup from behind the counter. In addition to being at the forefront of third-wave coffee in Paris, Télescope is a comfortable and friendly space where customers can meet and return to time and again. ◇

Vigårda

Stockholm's indoor BBQ

◊ Grilled food is usually associated with summertime picnics or backyard parties. But in Stockholm, Sweden, Melker Andersson, Danyel Couet, and Jonas Ålund have turned grilled meat and vegetables into something that can be had anytime of the year at their restaurant, Vigårda. These three cooks, who share a love of good food, had been thinking about opening a fast-food restaurant that served high-quality, locally-sourced fare. Their unusual solution was to fire up the grill and serve local meats and produce, which they cook fast, healthy, and fresh over a large charcoal grill.

Tawlet

Beirut's farmers' kitchen preserves grandma's local recipes

◇ Back to basics and with grandmother's unparalleled, homey recipes—such is the concept behind Tawlet, the latest venture from Kamal Mouzawak, Lebanese founder of Souk El Tayeb. A must-stop on a foodie tour of Beirut's restaurants, Tawlet is a farmers kitchen that features only the best artisan foods. The collective gathers cooks (or rather a bunch of life-trained grandmothers) from different regions and villages to promote traditional dishes, unite communities, and support sustainable agriculture. Want to travel north to Tripoli? Order a kibbeh stuffed with eggplant mousse, a kafta in yogurt sauce, a wheat berry and chicken casserole (requiring five hours on the stove), and a dandelion salad. For those in love with the Bekaa Valley, Tawlet Ammiq relays the same philosophy outside of the city, in Ammiq, a village partly destroyed by an earthquake in 1956, and nowadays protected as a biosphere reserve. "The project unfolds as a new way to rediscover forgotten villages through local food. It also sustains the local economy by supplying jobs for villagers and bringing to light their ancestral know-how through food heritage." Here, ◇ a resolutely vanguard eco-restaurant concept.

Pavé

Lounging with Milan's baker boys

The line between cafe and home is blurred at Milan's Pavé, where the comforting tastes and smells of home cooking create a meeting place with a relaxed and familiar atmosphere. Here, the smells of baked goods fresh out of the oven waft from the open kitchen into the seating area, which is decorated to feel more like a living room than a public space. In addition to baking its own breads, pastries, and cakes, Pavé serves sandwiches and coffee to customers who come for the events it hosts, or just to read or socialize in a place where food is equated with home.

Little Nap Coffee Stand

The grandness of a small but dedicated coffee place

◊ Tokyo's Little Nap Coffee Stand serves some of Japan's best coffee from an exceptionally small space. Located across from a quiet park, regulars and tourists seek out the Little Nap Coffee Stand for its excellent coffee. They also appreciate the attention paid to the details, including simple but cozy design, a quality selection of baked goods, good music on the stereo, and a welcoming atmosphere. Owner and music-lover Daisuke, along with a friend, roasts the cafe's beans, offering single-origin drip coffee as well as espresso-based drinks.

Little Nap
COFFEE
STAND

AUTUMN

SWE

Lapp & Fao

Chocolate books of Lapp & Fao

Whenever Linvard Bo Lapp and his partner Ephraim Fao travel the world in search of sweet delicacies from faraway places, they like to sit down at the end of a long day and record their thoughts and experiences in a diary. In turn, the diary provides them with valuable inspiration for their unusual chocolate creations. These records are now available as Lapp & Fao Chocolate Books. Only for the Future designed each chocolate bar to look like a diary, containing the essence of Lapp & Fao's travels as a delicious souvenir.

PACIFIC FUSION

HILLY VESPA RIDE

WHITE FLOE

Pinaki Studios

Edible Surfaces

Erik Spande and Leslie Vanderleeuw are the co-owners of the Amsterdam chocolate shop Chocolátl, which sells eclectic, premium sweets. Struck by the parallel processes of chocolate artisans and textile makers, they partnered with Arantza Vilas of the creative textile studio Pinaki Studios to create Edible Surfaces. The project, which draws its inspiration from textile manipulations like pleating, creasing, and embossing, presents the chocolates next to the textile pieces that inspired them, and is sponsored by Rococo Chocolates.

Rocambolesc Gelateria

The fabulous ice cream factory

◇ Joan, Josep, and Jordi Roca are the three brothers behind Catalonia's playful El Celler de Can Roca restaurant. Their newest addition to the family is an ice cream parlor that also sells books, perfumes, and a variety of candies and desserts. Youngest brother Jordi, who is in charge of desserts at El Celler de Can Roca, worked together with the Barcelona design studio Sandra Tarruella Interioristas to give the interior the feeling of a fantasy world. Customers can choose from six flavors of ice cream accompanied by butter cookies, cotton candy, and fresh fruit. The ice creams are all freshly made with natural products and ingredients from the recipes of El Celler de Can Roca.

Marije Vogelzang

Designing food experiences

Self-proclaimed eating designer Marije Vogelzang notes that because food is already perfectly designed by nature, she prefers to design food experiences that help people interact, explore, and engage. Her work includes projects such as Bits 'n' Bites at the Boijmans van Beuningen Museum, where a low-tech conveyor belt transported food and written messages to participants. HEADSPACE accompanied a symposium at Parsons The New School for Design and the Museum of Modern Art in New York, in which Vogelzang was asked to become an "accidental perfumer" and explore the fields of scent and design. She served bite-sized portions of food on a wall for the Eating Off the Wall event, and transformed the Zaha Hadid Fire Station at the Vitra Campus in Germany into a bakery that produced 2,500 loaves of Bastard Bread. These special loaves, which were a combination of the German, Swiss, and French breads of the region, spelled out sentences of love and affection on the fire station walls.

Scientific exploration of Nordic food roots

If Noma has been, for the past two years, on the top of every international food critics' list, the future of food is definitely being written a few steps away from the restaurant at the Nordic Food Lab. Founded by Noma's chef René Redzepi and food entrepreneur Claus Meyer—both founders of the New Nordic Cuisine—the lab is moored on a converted houseboat on the Copenhagen docks. A place fit for all kinds of experiments, it naturally welcomes water baths, centrifuges, and conical flasks complete with real kitchen appliances including steel surfaces, ovens, and chopping boards. The father of modern-day foraging, Redzepi is known for his free-form approach and studious investigation into the culinary possibilities of foraged, Nordic ingredients. Together with the Nordic Food Lab, he published "Guidelines for Sustainable Foraging," which mixes common sense with practice and a sharp eye for healthy, natural sites.

If many chefs have merely surfed on the trend of going local, Redzepi has made it a strict rule to use only local products. In reality, it means that Spanish ham, Italian olive oil, or even lemons are not allowed on the menu, and need to be replaced by Scandinavian alternatives such as wild berries, native seaweeds, Limefjord oysters, and rather unknown North Sea species like periwinkles and limpets (perhaps the abalone of the North), hand-dived arctic urchins, or Faroese langoustine. Run by Ben Reade, Head of Culinary Research and Development, the lab digs deep into new food experiments, unknown flavors, and recipes that "create cornerstones for a new kind of cuisine." Recently, the Nordic Food Lab has been focusing on fermentation and the microbiological research associated with it, but also on more complex, sensory driven interactions. "We've been conducting experiments to assess how sounds and colors and different perceptions affect a meal; for example, research shows that hearing can also affect the way food tastes. A lot of chefs are starting to take this into consideration, like at The Fat Duck, where we did an experiment with headphones—one could hear the sound of chips crunching while eating—which affected how crispy the food tasted. There is so much we can glean from scientific research.

We are always looking for new implements for our toolbox or new techniques to build up our culinary vocabulary so we can make the experience better for everyone," a Nordic Food Lab chef explains.

The research on new umami flavors derived from seaweed, conducted by Lars Williams, former Culinary R&D Emeritus for the Nordic Food Lab, is almost philosophical, even spiritual, and it has been embraced by the gastronomic community. What are we talking about? The term umami was coined by Japanese chemist Kikunae Ikeda back in 1908 to signify a unique and savory taste sensation that should be ranked as the fifth basic taste after the four classical modalities: sour, sweet, salty, and bitter. Following this path, Lars Williams identified and fine-tuned the use of novel ingredients to infuse a range of dishes such as ice cream, fresh cheese, and bread with umami taste. If scientists talk about breakthroughs, this is definitively one in the gastronomic world.

On the more practical side of Nordic Food Lab's agenda is looking at how one can de-bitter a dish. For example,

juice from endives is quite bitter, but can be successfully de-bittered using an ash solution. How does one come up with such a solution? By relying on as many resources as possible, and sometimes by revisiting old techniques. In a sociology journal, one of the team members read about an ancient North American Indian way of cooking corn with ash (scientifically called nixtamalization) to de-bitter it. Applying this technique to other ingredients produced some great results and the Nordic Food Lab suddenly became an expert in the field.

So, is the Nordic Food Lab looking at the future of food from a chemist-physicist's point of view? "Well yes and no. Our starting point and final goal always remain produce and taste," Reade explains. "But chefs are increasingly interested in science. They are more and more curious about what is actually happening in terms of physical and chemical senses when they are cooking. It has become important for them to have an understanding of the fundamental basics to perfect, repeat, or generate a novel approach."

Malle W. Trousseau

The world's best kitchen utensils to cut, cook, and contain

◊ Inspired by the Slow Food movement, Malle W. Trousseau compiles indispensable, uniquely crafted, and sustainable kitchen utensils. They are objects made by traditionally skilled craftsmen, or ingenious tools made by small-scale producers, and even rare objects exclusively created for the occasion. Culled from around the world, the collection includes an apron made by a saddler in Thônes, a Corsican or Japanese cutting knife, a Swedish spice grinder, Swiss vegetable peelers, and Finnish cast-iron casseroles. Acting as an amateur or expert's cooking trunk, not only does Malle W. Trousseau carefully hand-pick some of the best tools, but they come up with a definitive selection of 43 essential kitchen objects made to last a lifetime. Separated into three trays, ◊ these perfect gifts include all you need to cut, cook, and contain.

Salt Cellar, Oil Can, Oil Platter—reshaping food tools and eating experiences

Back in the day, American designer Charles Eames used to say: "The details are not the details. They make the product." Dutch designer Aldo Bakker endorses that belief with his collection of copper and porcelain products that range from a mixing bowl or soy pourer to a sauce pan and snakelike watering can. Sculpted in a seemingly simple, but subtly complex shape, each tableware object is entirely defined by how it will be used.

For example, "the Milk Jug pours from the side, not the top, to avoid dust collecting on the surface. The rim of the Salt Cellar varies in height to ensure that the salt disperses evenly. The Olive Oil Platter is designed to rub oil gently onto bread, rather than risk it drowning in oil," the designer explains. Taking the design a step beyond pure functionalism, Aldo Bakker imagines objects that comfortably nestle in the user's hand to make the experience all the more unique and tactile.

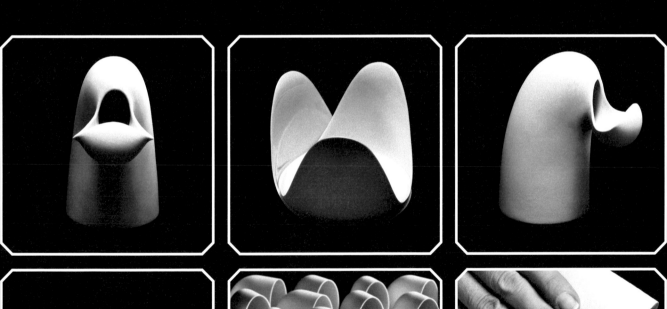

Parisian sweet art, created by a German

◊ After many years of living in France, Nina Junghans developed a love and appreciation for its macarons—and it's in France that she learned the craft of making this meringue-based confection. When she returned home to Germany, her passion traveled with her, today continuing to thrive at Art Sucré in Berlin. Here she uses her knowledge and skills as a pastry chef to give the people of Berlin the best of these sought-after sweets, including flavors such as the Provence-inspired Macaron Albertine (apricot-rosemary), Macaron Marilyn (tangerine and mint), and Macaron Wu (beet
◊ root and wasabi).

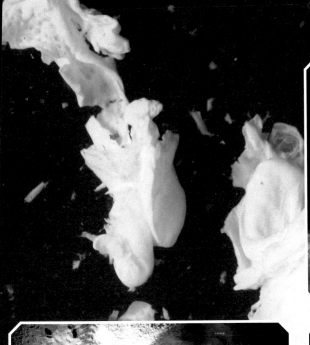

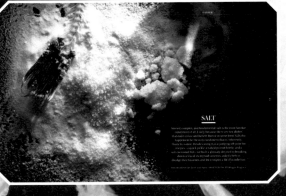

Gather Journal

Stunning images meet recipes for great meals

◊ Most food and lifestyle magazines are consumed and then forgotten when the next month's issue arrives. Gather Journal is a different kind of magazine, created to have staying power on the bookshelf with content that is a continual source of inspiration. Using a combination of stunning images, recipes, and words, Gather Journal inspires great meals as well as good atmosphere. Its founders, former NYLON fashion editors Michele Outland and Fiorella Valdesolo, use their experience and their passion for food to create this biannual publication, which is unusual not only for its beautiful and thoughtful content but also for the unique theme of each issue, which ties the content together in subtle ways. ◊

Carpaccio poetry

◊ Intrigued by how food is enhanced by the senses,
designer Hadar Kruk looks for connections between
food and how it's served to create a series of dishes
that enhance the sensory experience of food.
Each dish represents a different sense, such as the
hand-blown cocktail glass that is integrated with
a scented cork element to add to the taste of the
cocktail. The silicon in the tube dish is inspired by
piping bags, which allow the user to press down on
the dish and feel its contents. The hollow ceramic
body of the bowl makes the sound of ocean waves
◊ when the bowl is moved in a certain way.

Changing the perception of eating insects

If the folks behind Ento have their way, fresh grasshoppers will soon be available to purchase (and eat!) from your local grocery store. This small collective of postgraduate design students first thought about eating insects while researching solutions to global food security. In contrast to the resource-hungry livestock industry, they discovered that insects are a sustainable source of protein and nutrients—seen as inedible in Western culture. Ento made it their mission to change that perception by designing a new food culture around insects. The project includes a full-spectrum campaign from branding and accessible recipes to working with suppliers and distributors who can help make insects appetizing to Western palates, ultimately becoming part of the solution to accelerating global food demands.

Studio Appétit

Look who's eating

◇ We have all watched our dining companions eat from across the table, but watching ourselves eat is an illuminating if not awkward experience. The Eating Reflections installation asks participants to eat various foods in front of a mirror, allowing them to reflect on what they look like when they eat. New York City-based Studio Appétit is the creation of Ido Garini, a designer who specializes in food design. Born in Israel, he studied product design and culinary arts in various schools around the world. This experience gave him a deep appreciation of the culinary arts, which launched his career creating food-related projects, installations, and objects. This includes handcrafted and industrially manufactured dishes, edible food displays, large-scale eating installations, lectures, and workshops. ◇

Wohlfarth Schokolade

Spinning sweet records

Seldom do objects like vinyl records or salami have anything to do with chocolate—except in the work of Berlin-based chocolatier Christoph Wohlfarth, who invites consumers to see chocolate in a new way. His edible works of art include a chocolate record ready for the turntable, a very realistic chocolate salami, and handmade, paper-thin sticks accented by crystalline sea salt. Even his take on the standard hot chocolate has a unique spin: instead of dried cocoa powder, he adds shavings of Ecuadorian chocolate to steamed milk.

Comedian
Harmonists

*Mein kleiner grüner
Kaktus*

WOHLFARTH

NO PARKING

DOORS IN CONSTANT USE

Velopresso

Coffee on the go

◇ When Finnish designer Lasse Oiva and London designer Amos Field Reid combined their three favorite things—coffee, cycling, and sustainability—the result was the award-winning Velopresso, an off-the-grid mobile espresso bar powered by the pedal. Velopresso creates fine coffee with no electricity, no motors, and no noise by fusing human power with sensory pleasures, old and new technology, engineering, and aesthetics. The result is an innovative mobile coffee machine that works off the grid ◇ to sell quality espresso with a compact footprint.

Aveqia

Eating out and cooking together

◊ Sweden's forests, lakes, and seas have
always fostered its culinary traditions.
These natural resources provide diverse
offerings of regional ingredients—including wild mushrooms, berries, game, and
fish—that have inspired many Swedish chefs,
including Johan Kadar and David Berggren.
The two entrepreneurs opened Aveqia in
Stockholm as a restaurant and gathering
space with a unique concept: let people
get to know each other through active cooking, in which they prepare and eat a meal
together. This method of connecting people
through food was so popular that they
recently expanded to London.
◊

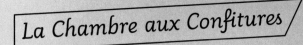

La Chambre aux Confitures

The treasury of jams, marmalades, and chutneys

In pre-war Paris, Lise Bienaimé's great-grandfather sold jams and pickled fruits and vegetables from his storefront shop. Decades later, Bienaimé quit her job in marketing at a large Paris company to join in the tradition of her great-grandfather. Her shop, La Chambre aux Confitures, is a delicatessen dedicated to artisanal jams, marmalades, and chutneys. Designed by Noël Dominguez, the shop is organized by season to emphasize the stars of each harvest, including winter citrus fruits and summer red and yellow fruits. Savory spreads like foie gras, chutneys, and salty jams are also available.

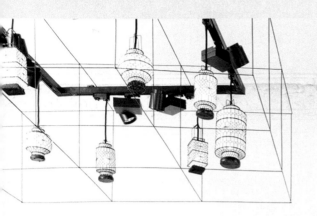
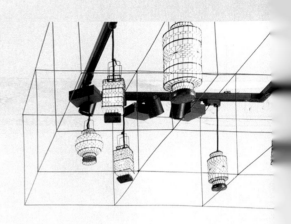

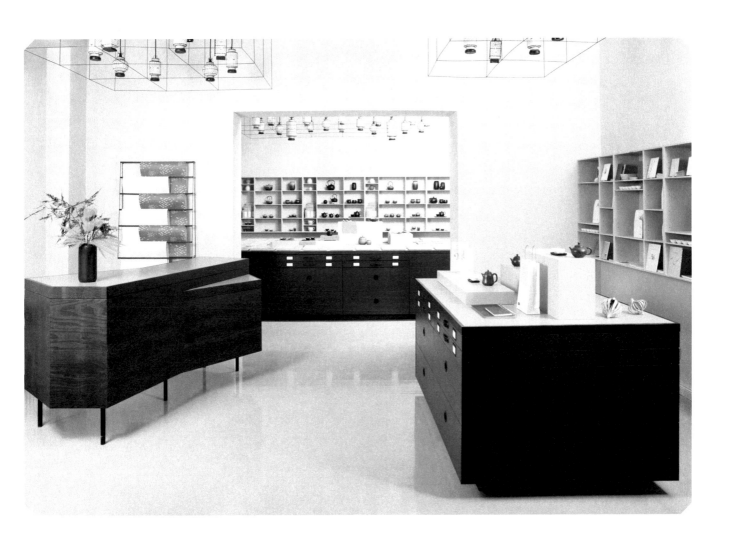

Paper and Tea

The Berlin temple of tea

For a very long time and across cultures, tea has been associated with vitality, mental balance, creativity, social activity, and communication. Catering to what we all crave, P & T brings us tea culture in the broadest sense. Living up to the core of the concept store strategy, P & T introduces a sensory, interactive approach. Guided by the mission to make sophisticated tea culture more accessible and rewarding to a broader audience, P & T's founder Jens de Gruyter decided to waive the conventional over-the-counter shop model in favor of an open presentation system, which encourages the customer to freely browse, smell, try, and discover the broad range of fine specialty teas. Enjoying the consultancy of staff tea experts and on-demand demonstrations at one of P & T's Gongfu-style tasting stations, the customers are invited to experience contemporary tea culture and reaffirm for themselves its power to fuel vitality, creativity, and communication.

Kitchen by Mike

Home is where the heart is

After Sydney chef Mike McEnearney worked abroad for the most sought-after chefs—think Joël Robuchon, Gordon Ramsay, Terence Conran—and was appointed as head chef of award-winning restaurant Rockpool, he started setting up pop-up dinners at French industrial design shop Ici et La, before establishing his new gourmet headquarters in a rough industrial warehouse in Rosebury, Sydney. There, the vast open cafe is a stage in itself. Grab an enamel plate, point to the salads or daily delicacies you want to sample, and wave to McEnearney as he pulls crisp golden suckling pig out of the oven. Pick a table on which covers are stacked in large tins of tomato puree. A democratic canteen in an upcoming neighborhood, Kitchen by Mike tells us a lot about our contemporary food culture. Today, it is about organic, home-baked, convivial, unfussy, and hearty food. Soon, Garden by Mike will be complete, where fresh herbs will be grown for the Kitchen.

Coffee Supreme

Coffee culture's third wave reaches New Zealand and Australia

◇ After many trips to visit the coffee growers they work with, the folks at Coffee Supreme know firsthand the care, consideration, and hard work that goes into growing great coffee. Over the years, they have made it a priority to establish strong relationships all along the coffee-making process, with coffee growers and exporters, roasters and cafe owners, and all the way to consumers. The result is a business that supplies cafes across New Zealand and Australia with beans of the highest quality, which have been carefully roasted to ensure that the inherent flavor potential comes through in each cup.

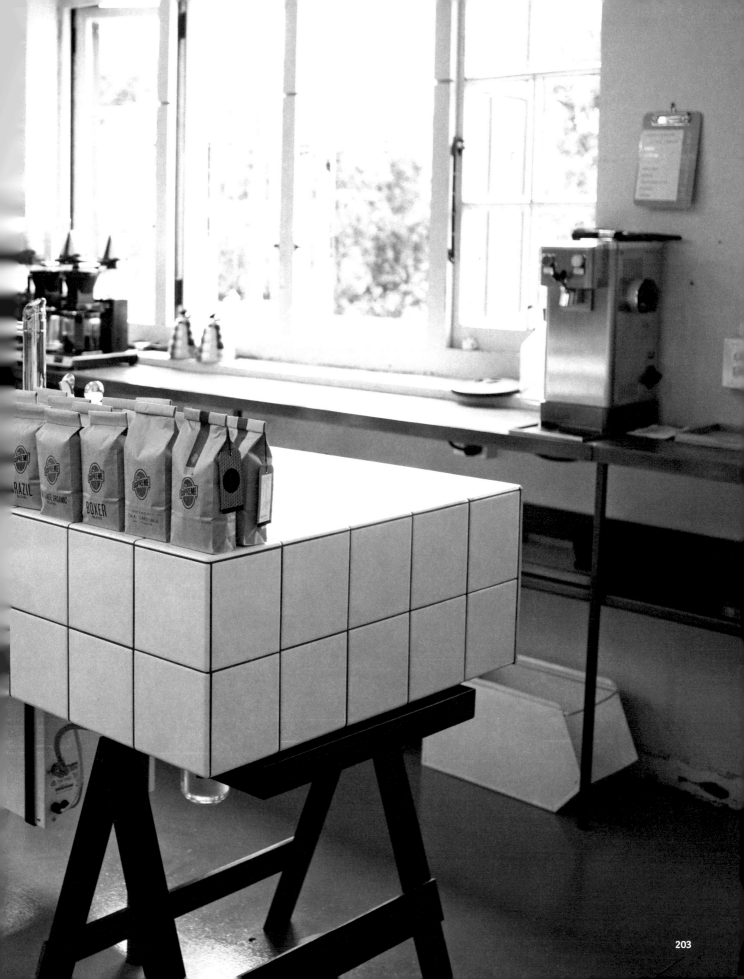

Food for thought

There are two types of food designers: those who are chefs and focus on the shape of what they serve, and those who are trained designers, who, with a passion for food but not necessarily any knowledge about cooking, use food as a material to create. Halfway in between, one finds Martí Guixé, a visionary oddball who has been in the food world since the nineties. He hates form but loves food, and isn't interested in the final product, but in its nutritional value.

Known as the Father of Spanish Food Design, Guixé has always seen design as a dynamic platform. His inclination for materials that are quick, readily available, and oriented toward mass consumption has led him, over the years, to become an important innovator in food design. In a nutshell, the ex-Droog designer hates the diktat of stylized objects and form and would rather concentrate on the social, almost anthropological attributes of a dish. It was he who began to question the sacred Spanish ritual of tapas, putting the bread inside the tomato instead of under it so that it could be eaten in front of the computer with just one hand. As society evolves, so should our food. Working with edible projects, as Guixé likes to name them, he looks around him, like a sociologist would, to adapt food to new lifestyles. As our lives become nomadic, our food follows. Hence the international trend of mobile food trucks pooling around densely populated urban centers at lunchtime. Food design should be about inventing solutions that cater to our ever-changing needs. Like us, food has become more ergonomic, functional, communicative, and informative even. Martí Guixé's I-cakes for example are iced on the top to show the exact proportion of each of the cake's ingredients, presenting those proportions as a physical pie chart and turning decoration into information. In one of his latest projects, the Lapin Kulta Solar Kitchen Restaurant, which was awarded the Innovative Media Prize and Special Prize for Innovative Marketing at the Vuoden

LAPIN KULTA

SOLAR
KITCHEN
RESTAURANT

OPENING DAYS:
SUNNY DAYS

Huiput awards in Finland, Marti Guixé looked at how a solar-powered kitchen affects food processing when cooking. Faced with a time sequence that is much more progressive, or changes continuously, solar-cooking impacts the taste and texture of prepared food in a surprising and positive way, bringing about a completely different tasting experience. As a nature-driven kitchen, it also highlighted our modern need for flexibility and immediacy. "It was all about testing people's flexibility; if it rains, we have to learn to be flexible, adapt, reschedule and deal with delays, all subject to nature. Of course information in real time was also important, as a cloud could ruin a business lunch. We learned that immediacy in information, decisions, and movements was crucial, and that the Lapin Kulta Solar Kitchen Restaurant's main goal was to rethink the perception of the kitchen, of cooking, and of food, all in relation to nature," Martí Guixé recalls.

Food vs. product? Product vs. food? The fact that our food is being turned into product—sometimes to the benefit of taste, sometimes against it—is definitely an underlying reflection in Martí Guixé's work. Turning his attention to food rather than objects, the designer sees food design as a way to reevaluate and redesign food, the industry, and the consumer. "I am only interested in food, as I consider it a mass consumption product and I like the fact that it is a product that disappears—by ingestion—and is transformed into energy.

And if you consider it bluntly, food has, for many years, no longer been a necessity but a consumer product. Looking ahead, Guixé firmly believes that "in forty years, food will have no shape or flavor: it will be nutritional and, more importantly, the table will not exist anymore."(1)

After the consumerism and information decades, the next one will embrace food in regard to the body and high-quality nutrition; it will focus on how one cooks, processes, and energizes food. "This will be the era when performance surpasses texture and taste in terms of importance, when the most urgent objective will be understanding the effects food has on our bodies."(1) "I might, perhaps, buy two chairs in my lifetime but I buy food three times a day," Guixé always says in a provoking way, proving, once again, that the future of food isn't about consumerism and form, but substance.

(1)   Quote from an interview published in finedininglovers.com in June 2011.

Terroir Parisien by Yannick Alléno

The Parisian way of French cuisine

◇ When introducing his Terroir Parisien book, three-Michelin-star chef Yannick Alléno went back to the roots of French cuisine to create innovative dishes from exceptional Parisian ingredients. Teaming up with farmers, cress growers, market gardeners, breeders, and beekeepers, he revived the secular traditions of one of France's richest agricultural regions. Familiar with saffron from Le Gâtinais, mint from Milly-la-Forêt, Houdan chicken, or the leafy purple ball of Pontoise cabbage? Did you know that the Normandy sole was first served in the early 1830s at a restaurant on Rue Montorgueil? Be prepared to. With unearthed old-fashioned produce in hand, Alléno has set for himself the task of reawakening old, forgotten, or obsolete recipes by adapting them to today's tastes. Moreover, he tries to imagine what Parisian cuisine would
◇ have become if it hadn't been abandoned.

Traveling across a world of food on the back of local ingredients

◊ In Montreal, the Société des Arts Technologiques acts as an interdisciplinary hub of digital culture. Part restaurant, part culinary lab, its recently launched Labo Culinaire, or Foodlab, ties together a rough industrial setting with high stools, a vast open-kitchen, and a rooftop terrace. Far from using molecular techniques, which a food lab always tends to suggest, local co-chefs Seth Gabrielse and Michelle Marek fight menu boredom above all. Putting together a small menu that changes every two weeks, they use local ingredients to showcase the best of regional cuisines. Come one week for a Russian Easter and return the next for Spanish grilled calamari and chorizo on a ragout of chickpeas, making your taste buds travel to Sevilla. Later in the year, one is surprised by how Canadian organic produce and Mediterranean wines crafted by small producers perfect a Middle Eastern mezze platter. In the heart of Montreal, embark on a world tour of what almost seems like local flavors. ◊

Taking time for tea

Drinking tea is a relaxing ritual in Japan and the Middle East, where the beverage fulfills important social roles in addition to quenching thirst. Noting that many people in Western cultures drink tea in a rush, and often from an old mug, designer Femke Roefs sought to develop a system that would make it a more enjoyable experience. The Tea Cabinet is a bamboo tea trolley with room for a handcrafted copper kettle, heat source, cups, saucers, sweets, and teas. It can be wheeled to the garden, the couch, or the dinner table so that each cup of tea can become part of a special moment.

Three-star pub food

◇ Rule-breaking, unusual experiments, and an exploding oven:
Heston Blumenthal's journey to creating a three-star Michelin
restaurant in a 450-year-old pub has been an unconventional one. In between falling in love with cooking at age
16 and being awarded best restaurant in the world in 2005,
Blumenthal taught himself the classical repertoire of French
cuisine at night and visited France each summer to learn
every aspect of gastronomy from restaurants, suppliers,
and wine estates. He opened The Fat Duck in 1995 and began
to explore multi-sensory perception, science, subjective
perceptions of flavor, history, and how they can be applied to
◇ cooking and food.

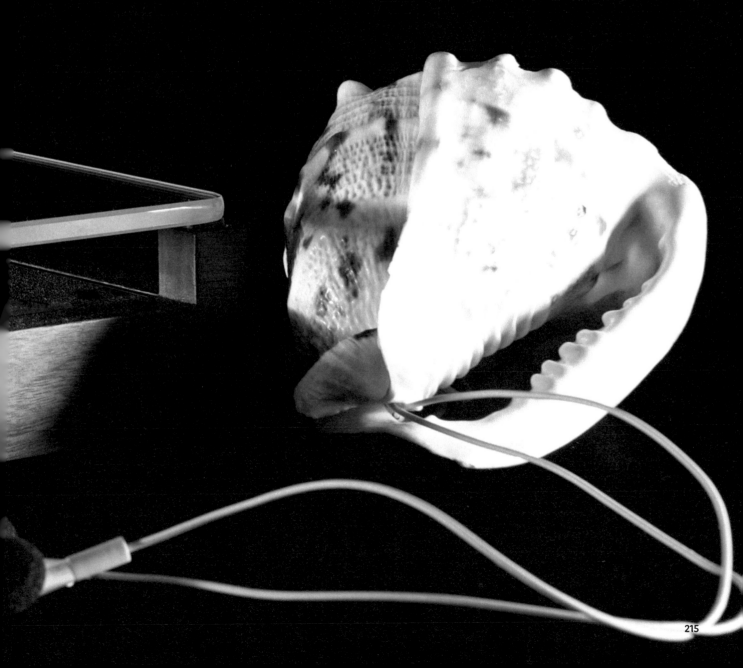

Global Feast

Olympic nations around one table

◊ International spirit is the soul of the Olympics. Looking for a way to celebrate the 2012 London games and bring people together from all over the world, Underground Supper Club chef Kerstin Rodgers and architect Alex Haw decided to turn to food. Their pop-up restaurant Global Feast offered 20 nights of cuisine prepared by an international roster of top supper club chefs. Each evening was hosted by a different chef who served a menu that celebrated international delicacies. The Global Feast table included a global landscape as its centerpiece and seating for 80 guests along its coastlines, which were illumi-
◊ nated by city lights.

Learning the language of your senses

Designed to demystify the process of vinification, The Blocks event encouraged visitors to discover and awaken their palate using sight, touch, smell, and taste. Trained sommeliers took guests on a journey through five wooden totems inspired in form by the five groups of grapes available for tasting. Each contained different bespoke scents produced for the event in conjunction with a perfumer, and were designed to help guests choose wines to suit their personal palate. Not satisfied with stimulating only the nose, Studio Toogood worked with designers to create glass cabinets filled with highly visual, poetic interpretations of the terminology associated with describing wine by artists and designers. To complete the gastronomic experience, guests were seated under canopies of illuminated glass grapes on Faye Toogood's iconic aluminum Spade Chair, which was cold to the touch to remind guests of their cellar-like experience.

The art of drinking

Staying off the map. Flying under the radar. The new trend in luxury living is all about staying anonymous. And there is no major city today without a new speakeasy bar that hides in a dark corner at the end of a narrow alley. With a secret entrance inside the hot dog joint Crif Dogs on St. Mark's Place, New York's Please Don't Tell bar naturally filters out those who aren't in the know. Led by mixologist Jim Meehan, Please Don't Tell opened in 2007 in what used to be a Japanese bubble tea lounge, right at the moment when the cocktail revolution started hitting the underground bar scene. "The entrance through the phone booth rather than out front wasn't designed to be cool, it was just our only option if we didn't want to file a request for a separate liquor license," Meehan recalls. Like in the good old prohibition days, bending the rules and avoiding the scrutiny of the administration was key to the success of this venture. "Having a nondescript door is definitely what comes to mind when I think of speakeasies. And when Please Don't Tell opened, although a few really good speakeasy bars were well in place, it suddenly felt like we had coined a trend. But we didn't pioneer it," he adds. "And the most interesting thing is that, when you look at the bar from a cocktail historian's point of view, we weren't speakeasy. Speakeasies were illegal bars that served bootlegged or adulterated hooch, they didn't serve culinary cocktails. So we became 'modern speakeasy,'" Meehan explains.

First, Jim Meehan started running his bar like a restaurant. "We've forged our own definition of bar hospitality; the way we run the bar is the way a restaurant runs its dining room, meaning there is no standing and there is enough staff to serve you." Then, Please Don't Tell has a cocktail menu that changes regularly. Some have become classics while others reflect a taste for a certain type of cocktail at a given moment in time. As a whole, the bar and menus are never static, as they evolve according to seasons, ingredients, and friends' taste. "It's a home base for exploration and social interaction. Plus, the drinks I've served have always evolved over time," he says. Although Please Don't Tell became popular over the years, its secret is that it was never run as a popular place. There has never been this urge to redecorate; it's always found a new breath through the quality of people that come to share more than just a drink. The art of a great cocktail, the culture of its bartenders, the level of service, and the quality of the crowd all diverge from mainstream business models, and the success of many speakeasies is precisely to defy business models. Passionate mixologists go their own way, buy and craft expensive liquors, close their doors to the masses, refuse hipsters, talk in codes, and sometimes even refuse to have a printed menu. The taste of old bitters, the smell of chalk on blackboards, the soft patina of an old leather couch, and the retro outfit of a bartender wearing a bowtie are some of the quintessential attributes of a modern speakeasy bar.

Unleashing the wild expert that sleeps inside him, Jim Neehan speaks of a cocktail that he's always served at

Please Don't Tell as he would about a passionate love story: a love story called The Mezcal Mule. "This drink has muddled cucumber, house-made ginger beer, passion fruit juice, lime juice, single-village mezcal, and cayenne. There's sour from the lime and the passion fruit, spice from the ginger beer, strength and smoke from the spirit, a floral and vegetal quality from the cucumber, and heat from the cayenne. So when made properly, it's a drink that is strong, sweet, sour, floral, smoky, and hot. I've always said cocktails are not vehicles to get drunk, although they are intoxicating. Here, you're getting a flavor experience in the same way that you do when you're eating at, say, a great restaurant. You're not eating to get full, you're eating to see what the chef is doing." And he continues: "Some cocktails are more than drinks: they will always

remain vivid memories. I'll always remember my first cocktail at Milk & Honey bar. There was no menu; they asked you what spirit you liked, what style of drink you liked, and then they brought me a Goldrush. I'll never forget this antique cocktail tray with a candle on it. Then came this thick weird dental napkin onto which a frozen double Old Fashioned glass with a giant cube of hand-cut ice was placed. There was also a stainless steel iced tea straw which had been cut perfectly to fit the glass, and I realized, 'I've been serving cocktails for almost eight years and I've never had a cocktail like this.'" He recalls this perfectly, knowing that in the art of mixing cocktails there is always room for exhilarating surprises.

Celebrating classic cocktail culture

Hidden behind a few stairs on New York City's trendy Elizabeth street, The Daily has something of a Prohibition-era feel. To outfit the interior, designers AvroKO chose polished leather booths, dim yellow lights, vintage postcards, retro-typography, and a floor-to-ceiling felted wall that features the ever-changing daily menus. But most of all, The Daily has a serious cocktail culture. Tinctures and bitters line the bar, sleek ice chunks wait to be shaved, fresh fruit is garnished, and apothecary-like shelves of mason jars are filled with all manners of mixological wonders. Changing every day, as its name suggests, the cocktails come with a twist or historic pedigree, topped with a shiso leaf, or with a creative denomination like the Algonquin, which blends rye, Vermouth, and pineapple, as typed on the blackboard.

Scrap Lab – Linda Monique

Upcycling leftovers
into glamorous food experiences

◇ As a chef, food designer, stylist, and the Director of CREAM, a
creative marketing consulting agency based in Melbourne,
Australian Linda Monique is a culinary oddball. A genuine glo-
betrotter, she defines her cooking as a mixture of Japanese
and French, with undertones of Middle Eastern and British
classic items. "I like to play with cultures." Her personal food
blog receives over 100,000 hits annually, and Monique recently imagined Scrap Lab for boutique hotel Andaz Liverpool
Street. After a three-month study of how to upcycle and
reinvent ingredients, she designed this series of experiential
dinners, utilizing only food byproducts and leftovers such
as sea bass cheeks or roasted off cuts. "For me, Scrap Lab
exemplified the bipolar opposite of the luxury norm; it went
against the association of luxury hotels with sole opulence.
Further down the line, it redefines hotel dining and gives
precedence to establishing sustainable food systems within
◇ mass food & beverage operations," Linda explains.

Journey on the Table

◇ Food artist Ayako Suwa and her team at Food Creation avail themselves of everyday life to create culinary experiences of astonishing variety. Drawing much inspiration from nature ("the feeling of sand running through the fingers, the smell of rain on warm stone"), they looked into the behavior of migratory birds to create the Journey on the Table. The result of a month-long intense collaboration with the creative cooking sanctuary 2am:lab, this multisensory experience dinner took the guests on a culinary adventure from the lake to the grassland, through the forest, and across city to ocean.
◇

Teatime Production

Orchestrating a culinary extravaganza

◊ Big parties are Teatime's first love, but this specialty event producer organizes press-worthy, on-brand experiences on all scales, from the intimate to the monumental. These epic affairs pair food and drink with commissioned performances such as an interactive, Hitchcock-themed eating experience and a series of late-night dining events that feature six courses of playfully reworked traditional desserts. Teatime is run by Polly Betton, a former graphic designer and fashion shoot producer who made the leap into event production in 2008. Her production partners include Andrew Stellitano of Blanch & Shock and David Bradley from The
◊ Curious Confectioner.

New *Hitchpop Corn*

Mr. Hitchcocks Finest

Cinema
Hitch-Popping
Pop Corn
With added smoke!

Number 1 For That Smokey Taste

Combines Popcorn & Liquid Nitrogen

(for commercial use)

TRY

'HITCHPOPCORN'

FRESH AND SMOKEY

AVAILABLE AT THE
CONCESSION STAND

Pret a Diner: The Burlington Social Club

Michelin-star dishes and innovative cocktails find a temporary home in London's Royal Academy

Picture London Royal Academy's first-floor galleries and grand Senate Rooms staged with floor-to-ceiling scaffolding. A quick and impressive stage, set up to welcome Pret a Diner's newest high-flung foodie event, The Burlington Social Club features a unique social drinking and dining experience orchestrated around Michelin-star dishes and innovative cocktails. Putting the emphasis on the art of mixology, the venue welcomes renowned mixologists from across Europe, such as star bartenders Marian Beke and Stephan Hinz, to share the stage with inspired dishes, live music, and art installations designed by contemporary neon artist Olivia Steele. Enjoy a Coquetier, an eggshell filled with rum, pimento, chocolate, bitters, PX, protein, and cinnamon, paired with a serving of teriyaki ox cheeks with parsnip, local baby herbs, and orange, or, chicken skin and tofu panna cotta with sea bream sashimi, shimeji, and soy foam.

232

Avant-garde chefs meet local artisans

◇ Back to nature, to a sense of place—this is the concept behind Cook It Raw, an annual platform for the world's most avant-garde chefs to come together with traditional food producers and local artisans to explore the possibilities of cuisine in a remote location. It was founded in 2009 by chef Alessandro Porcelli, a culinary consultant based in Copenhagen, along with the help of journalist Andrea Petrini and René Redzepi. As a think tank of industry leaders, the inaugural group of chefs were brought together to discuss current issues affecting the world through the lens of food. Participants were pushed to consider the environment, culinary traditions, and the creativity within the regions they visited, working together as a team, ◇ with no egos.

The Cook It Raw gatherings have taken place in Lapland, Japan, Denmark, Italy, and most recently in the remote rural town of Suwalki in the forest bordering Lithuania. The annual gatherings encourage local hunters, artisanal producers, and foragers following ancestral paths to share their local heritage by teaching a dozen of the world's most sought-after chefs about indigenous treats. Cook It Raw looks first and foremost at food as untamed cultural heritage waiting to be tapped, unveiling family secrets and local delicacies such as smoked vendace (sielawa) or native herb honey in Poland, to name just a couple. These culinary meetings of the minds bring to the table a unique dining experience that encourages innovation, provides an arena for true exchange, and addresses social, cultural, and environmental issues.

Artists Index

A Delicious Life
NEW FOOD ENTREPRENEURS

This book was conceived, edited, and designed by Gestalten.

Edited by Sven Ehmann, Robert Klanten, and Marie Le Fort
Features and preface by Marie Le Fort
Project texts by Rebecca Silus and Marie Le Fort
Cover and layout by Hendrik Hellige
Cover photography clockwise from top left: Nicole Franzen
for Morris Kitchen, Kikuko Usuyama for Morris Kitchen, Ailine
Liefeld for Cemilzade Confiserie Orientale, Blaise Hayward for
Gasoline Alley
Typefaces: Calcine, Canary by Mark Froemberg
Foundry: www.gestaltenfonts.com

Project management by Pauleena Chbib
Production management by Martin Bretschneider
Proofreading by Rachel Sampson
Printed by Offsetdruckerei Grammlich, Pliezhausen
Made in Germany

Published by Gestalten, Berlin 2013
ISBN 978-3-89955-467-0

For more information, please visit www.gestalten.com.

Bibliographic information published by the Deutsche
Nationalbibliothek. The Deutsche Nationalbibliothek lists this
publication in the Deutsche Nationalbibliografie; detailed
bibliographic data are available online at http://dnb.d-nb.de.

None of the content in this book was published in exchange
for payment by commercial parties or designers; Gestalten
selected all included work based solely on its artistic merit.

This book was printed according to the internationally
accepted ISO 14001 standards for environmental protection,
which specify requirements for an environmental management system.

This book was printed on paper certified by the FSC®.

Gestalten is a climate-neutral company. We collaborate
with the non-profit carbon offset provider myclimate
(www.myclimate.org) to neutralize the company's carbon
footprint produced through our worldwide business
activities by investing in projects that reduce CO_2 emissions
(www.gestalten.com/myclimate).